NIMROD INTERNATIONAL JOURNAL

AWARDS 32

Spinning Legends... telling truths

Nimrod International Journal IS INDEXED IN
HUMANITIES INTERNATIONAL COMPLETE

ISBN: 0-9794967-6-4   ISSN: 0029-053X
Volume 54, Number 1
Fall/Winter 2010

THE UNIVERSITY OF TULSA — TULSA, OKLAHOMA

This issue of *Nimrod* is dedicated to

Daniel Marder
July 10th, 1923 — June 16th, 2010
former Chair of The University of
Tulsa's English Department
and member of the *Nimrod* Editorial Board

and

James G. Watson
June 16th, 1939 — March 30th, 2010
Frances W. O'Hornett Professor of Literature
of The University of Tulsa*

Fragile

We are all fragile.
There is no end to it:
The breaking and the need for repair,
The shattered glass, broken promises,
Crumbling walls and fences, hearts and bones —
All fragile! Carefully . . . oh so carefully . . .
We gather and meld fragments together.
They will break again, yet be stronger for the repair.
Our work is never done.

— FR

*See poem on page 168

ACKNOWLEDGEMENTS

This issue of *Nimrod* is funded by donations, subscriptions, and sales. *Nimrod* and The University of Tulsa acknowledge with gratitude the many individuals and organizations that support *Nimrod*'s publication, annual prize, and outreach programs: *Nimrod*'s Advisory and Editorial Boards; and *Nimrod*'s Angels, Benefactors, Donors, and Patrons.

ANGEL ($1,000+)
Margery Bird, Ivy & Joseph Dempsey, Stephani Franklin, The Herbert & Rosaline Gussman Foundation, Burt Holmes & Mary Lee Townsend, Susan & Bob Mase, Ruth K. Nelson, The John Steele Zink Foundation

BENEFACTOR ($500+)
Gary Brooks, Cynthia Gustavson, Bruce Kline, Donna O'Rourke & Tom Twomey, Lisa Ransom, Diane & James Seebass, Joy Whitman, Jane Wiseman, Randi & Fred Wightman

DONOR ($100+)
Sharon Bell & Gregory Gray, Harvey & Sandra Blumenthal, Phil Bolian, Colleen Boucher, Mary Cantrell & Jason Brimer, Harry Cramton, Marion & Bill Elson, Nancy & Ray Feldman, Joan Flint, Susan & William Flynn, Joseph Gierek & Mary Young, Sherri & Stuart Goodall, Helen Jo Hardwick, Ellen Hartman, Frank Henke III, Nancy Hermann, Carol Johnson, William Kellough, The Kerr Foundation, Marjorie & David Kroll, Lydia Kronfeld, Edwynne & George Krumme, Robert LaFortune, Mary & Robert Larson, Roberta & the late Daniel Marder, Geraldine McLoud, Melvin Moran, Rita Newman, Catherine Gammie Nielsen, Nancy & Thomas Payne, Judy & Roger Randle, Kate Reeves, Patricia & Gil Rohleder, Andrea Schlanger, Ann Daniel Stone, Fran & Bruce Tibbetts, Dorothy & Michael Tramontana, Renata & Sven Treitel, Melissa & Mark Weiss, The Kathleen Patton Westby Foundation, Ruth Weston, Marlene & John Wetzel, Michelle & Clark Wiens, Penny Williams, Josephine Winter, Maria & Yevgeny Yevtushenko, Rachel Zebrowski

PATRON ($50+)
M. E. Arnold, Margaret Audrain, Kimberly Doenges, F. Daniel & Kay Duffy, Laurie Fuller, Susan Gronberg, Maria Lyda, Darlene Rough, Joan & Harry Seay, Jyo Umezawa, Krista & John Waldron, Martin Wing

TABLE OF CONTENTS

FRANCINE RINGOLD

Editor's Note
Awards 32: Spinning Legends, Telling Truths

For the sake of a relaxed but tangible order and ease of approach, we have divided this award-winning anthology into three sections: *Spinning, Legends,* and *Truths.* Those who recognize the complexities of truth-telling know that we often spin out our days in a whirl of humor *and* tragedy. Simultaneity, not singularity, creates legends *and* tells truths (or, at least, shades of the truth.) The legend, a story, passed down for generations and presented as fact, actually turns, undergoes changes, each time it is retold—as does history itself. Witness the battle of Thermopylae, told by Greek historians Herodotus and Thucydides, and see the event from different sides of the field, and in a different light. In perspective, as National Book Award-winner Colum McCann says, the "great world spins," the legend and its truth grow and change. Consider James Valvis's "Big Georgia and the Sewer."

Then there is the matter of how direct and bold we wish to be as we tell what we feel to be the truth. As Emily Dickinson said: "Tell all the truth, but tell it slant . . ./Success in circuit lies . . . The Truth must dazzle gradually/Or every man be blind—".

Often a metaphor provides the "slant," the indirect approach to the truth, even as it expands the range of what might otherwise have been a bold simple assertion. The comparison of a state of mind or feeling to the concrete and tangible provides a mask—not to hide behind but—to speak through. "Chambered Nautilus, with Tinnitus and Linden" for example, in Terry Blackhawk's first prize-winning poem, contrasts the geometrical precision of nature in the Nautilus shell, as it moves onward in a spiral into larger and larger proportionate chambers, with the radical changes one faces in life. At the same time, nature's well-managed pattern gives us reassurance that, no matter how radical the change, there is a return to due proportion, "as we try to hold/the shell against the ear, to feel the reach/and return of one's pulse traveling/through a golden mean."

Jude Nutter's second-place poem, "My Mother's Teeth," speaks of the reality of illness and death more directly, while also creating a sense of calm and proportion through not only what it says but how it says it—the tight two- and three-line stanzas

x

holding in the grief and loss so that balance too is accepted as part of the truth of life and death and the recurring story of survival.

The spinning, the truth, is imbedded in the psyche of a young girl in Lydia Kann's honorable mention story, "The Arrival." When her mother suffers a severe breakdown, after years of struggling with mental illness, Lili/Lisa is sent across country, from the jungles of New York City to the alluring dystopia of California, to live with virtual strangers. Exiled from the protective role she has served taking care of her mother and herself since childhood, the girl, despite the spin she has been given about the land of milk and honey, finds the cultural transition a spiral into a fate like her mother's.

Sue Pace's "Obituary for an Asshole," another honorable mention in the 2010 *Nimrod* Awards competition, gives the reader glimpses of the narrator's own history as she struggles through versions of the obituary she has been assigned to write for her step- father. Each version attempts to refine the character of the deceased in order to create a legend for our time. Once again, it is the structure of the tale through which we discover the miracle of simplicity. Similarly, John Knoepfle's "Morning of Confused Purposes" speaks the truth with honesty and directness as it makes its elegant turns demonstrating how "all that is alive this day should lift us up."

"Really Good Feet," Laura LeCorgne's second prize-winning story, also winds its way through confusion and loss as it evokes the reality of family, in all its multiplicity, division and pain, facing the death of one sister and the emotionally frozen state of the other —while even the title injects an ironic note of humor into the panic and pain.

It is once again the telling of its truths, the distinctive ironic voice of Shannon Robinson's first prize story, "Miscarriages," that transforms the desperate and grueling search for a full-term birth into another of life's mixed metaphors. How fitting that the story ends with the legend of Persephone, mistress of the dark and the light.

As the bird coos in Harry Bauld's honorable mention poem, "Loft": *Go figure it out . . . Go figure it out!*

Our selection process:

Nimrod International Journal extends deep appreciation to all who submitted to the 2010 awards competition. There were 690 poetry manuscripts and 571 short stories submitted. Cover letters and names of authors were separated from the submissions before they were read and a number was assigned to each manuscript and corresponding cover letter. Selecting finalists from these 1,261 was a task that dominated the lives of 41 *Nimrod* editors all spring, as it has each year for the past 31 years. These generous and talented folks approached their mission with dedication and discretion, reading and rereading, comparing notes, and speaking for favorites. The finalists' manuscripts, still without cover letters or names, were sent to the judges for 2010, Molly Peacock, poetry, and David Wroblewski, fiction. They chose the winners and honorable mentions from the finalist group.

The additional selections in this issue were chosen from our vast store of "over-the-transom" submissions and acceptances during the year, including translations from the Turkish of Omur Caymaz and the German of Georg Trakl.

Kathryn Dunlevie, *Research*,
archival pigment print on panel, 8.5" x 8.5"

Kathryn Dunlevie, *Reforestation*,
archival pigment print on panel, 8.5" x 8.5"

Chambered Nautilus, with Tinnitus and Linden

Is it crickets, a thin wind across a wire,
hiss of spindrift off the crest of a wave,
or radio emissions from a planetary probe?
When I took the hearing test, this sound
I carry nearly drowned out the faint high or low-
pitched pulses of air I strained in order to "pass"
the test to hear—each tone becoming ever more
soft, so barely there I could almost see
it disappear—just as I've often strained
after birds in the farthest reaches
of the canopy.   Call it a squint of sound,
tone on the edge of not   existing at all
a hint, a sleight of   breath—   a flutter on the branch,
bare after-image of the spot from which
desire just—   took wing.
                              Dr. Seidman calls it
a phantom phenomenon—lost hearing
reminding the hearer of itself—lost sounds
trying to make themselves heard. I make them ghost
sounds, haunting neural tin-pan alleys where syn-
aptic nitty gritty saints go marching intra-
cellular-ly. Call it mitochondrial fizz,
call it not-so-good vibrations—bits of DNA
decoding, or decaying, along the dendrites tip-
tapping the cochlea.   It is static, uni-
linear, all pervasive in-
vasive, this persistent insistence.   I will color it
empty flat sizzle not to be tuned
out—or away.   But ah, to listen differently
to pick up and put back down again
the shell against the ear, to feel the reach
and return of one's pulse traveling

1

through a golden mean.   Shells do that, I mean —
arrange themselves in proportional beauty. Take
the Nautilus whose chambers catch and toss
back the rhythm of the wave — all heart and shush
echoing   yes   listen   really   it *does*   sound
like crickets.   So let us think again, of crickets,
yes again — and luminous evenings — and the beauty
of *again* again. How modest and mere those
myriad insects those summer nights our son
                    had just turned three.
There was music and a pulse to the background then.
And did it come from two hearts humming
                                  or the echo from
that tree we loved — the heart-shaped leaves
of the heart-shaped linden, with its pour
of pollen — a buzzing fragrance of blossoms
and in every one of them a bee.

Cookie Johnson, pencil drawing

The Lost Life List

Surely not the worst of my losses,
the places, species, dates—*Point Pelee, 5/7/93*—
Blue-gray Gnatcatcher—*Carolina Wren*—
all tucked inside a guidebook that is gone.

But when my friend asked which rare sighting
I "grieved most to lose" in order to put
my loss in her poem, I thought how grief
magnifies the smallest things—lips tight shut,
a single leaf in unsuspecting light—
and did not choose to share.

After I took her call, I went for a walk
by the river. It was a late October morning,
bathed in golden fog. The willows
were in perfect dying blaze, synchronous
with mist so thick it seemed to brew the light.

Who could see, let alone lose a bird
in such dense air? How be anything but lost
in that shimmering cloud?
                    From overhead,
beside the bayou at the far end of the island,
came a heavy, almost maritime crank:

the sound of the wings of swans in flight.
Their mechanical downbeats, so close above
but cloaked in fog—I neither saw nor lost them.
Nor did I lose the voices of men singing

as they fished in a foreign language—
and the boomboxes from picnic grounds
on the other side of the trees
seemed filled with intent to be found.

Litany of loss and leaves, tailor-made
for mulling. It was all trumpet and bass,
all poem and shine. It was endless,
forgiving, and I had already lost it,
even though it was mine.

I think of my ex-husband standing in sunlight

but it's a frozen tree frog I hold
in my hand, capturing the evening
sun as it slants through the palmettos.

He's hollowed, stiffened in position,
and I balance him on my desk top
poised and posed like a football lineman

ready for the hike. One leg stretches
twice the length of the forward-crouching
body making a stem I can twirl

between my fingers. The other forms
a Z, its toenails barely touching
the desk, as if he's about to spring.

Decay would not have left him so fixed
and exact, like a paper lantern
or a cicada's husk. Some abrupt

and thoroughgoing freeze must have caught
him thus, midstride, his claws still clinging
to the bark. Hold him up to the sun,

the spine's an x-ray, the skull a dark
spoon above half-closed eyes, crescent slits
admitting light. The dried pod of him

fairly glows, revealing veins, vessels
still red but no longer pulsing. I
wonder what he saw as the cold fell,

if the lids lowered as the blood slowed,
the abdomen puffed out, innards turned
to vapor and he became his shell.

Miscarriages

Again

You look familiar.

That is what the anesthesiologist says to me. She's petite, much younger than I expected, and has pale, smooth skin. I'm here to have a D&C. I had an abortion three years ago, but that was in another city. In a few minutes, this woman will take the clear plastic cup that she's now holding and place it over my nose and mouth; she will put me to sleep. I will have no memory of her doing so.

D&C is short for Dilation and Curettage. The initials are for delicacy as much as for convenience. It is the operation performed after a miscarriage, wherein the fetus (or dead baby, however you wish to think of it) is sucked out of your womb. A bit of vacuuming in preparation for the next tenant. If there will be one.

I don't have a reply for the anesthesiologist's remark, although I feel that I should. She sounds so casually certain. Oh, I say.

Maybe I just have one of those faces. I'm lying down on a padded table, dressed in a large, green two-ply paper gown. A hose attached to a circular notch on the gown blows in warm air, inflating me like a pool toy, making me feel both comforted and a little silly. I'm wearing purple socks, with teddy bears on them in a raised, rubberized pattern. The hospital provided them. These I will keep. I will wear them around the apartment for the next few days until the soles get dirty and I begin to worry about the state of the unswept floors.

The nurses have directed my husband, Sean, to another room that is filled with other patients' relatives, waiting. As a day-surgery patient, you're allowed to bring only one relative, and no children under twelve. So in other words, no children. We'd read that on the slip of paper given to me by the nurse at my pre-op examination two days ago.

I guess they don't want a bunch of crazy brats running around upsetting people, grinding cookies into the rug, Sean said, probably thinking of the sign we read on our first visit to the obstetrician's office, stating NO FOOD OR DRINKS. *But you can bring in that coffee, honey. It's got a lid*, the receptionist had told him as we hesitated in the doorway. Sean has an open kind of charm about him, so she probably would have let him bring in a melting popsicle.

Senbazuru

I had this notion, following my miscarriage, that I would undertake an origami project of folding a thousand paper cranes. In grade school, my class read a story about a brave Japanese kid who folded a thousand cranes while in hospital, hoping to get well. I remember feeling both impressed by and jealous of the kid's dignity. According to ancient lore, whoever folds a thousand paper cranes will be granted a wish. I imagined a cinematic time-passage montage, wherein people would see me, patiently creasing small pieces of paper, bending and unfolding with gentle, nimble precision. Tiny paper birds would accumulate in our apartment. White birds, birds with the faint blue lines of notebook paper, glossy magazine-scrap birds, birds folded from the silver paper discarded from cigarette packs. It would become a joke among my co-workers at the library and my friends, that this was my Zen fidget, my quiet party trick. And then, after I announced that I was pregnant, I could explain what was with the months of folding. I would have a mobile of paper cranes for the baby's crib, perhaps even a framed print of a crane—a white bird stretched in flight against a powder-blue background—that people would mistake for a stork. Later, I would tell my child the story of my ongoing dedication, how I humbly willed him or her into existence.

I sat at my desk, turned on my laptop and went online to learn how to fold a paper crane. I found a set of directions that consisted of diagrams showing a step-by-step transformation of a square of paper into a bird with pointy wings. It seemed simple enough, once I finally managed to cut a piece of paper into a perfect square (I've always found it difficult to cut straight lines). But as I started following the instructions, I could only get so far before I was stumped. I tried a different Web site, a different set of diagrams. Again, I had a problem. Again I tried a different Web site. But each set of directions I found seemed to leave out a crucial opening step, or depict one step in abstract terms (Where is that arrow pointing, exactly? What do they mean by *fold the outer corners to the center*? How?) The online videos I found featured people whose hands occasionally obscured their operations. I folded, re-folded, unfolded and rotated the paper, smoothing it out and push-ing aside the books and notes cluttering my desk so I had more space to work, but I just couldn't replicate any of the instructions beyond a certain point. I left my creased not-crane by the laptop. A paper diamond. A crumpled kite.

The kid in that story—I think she died at the end, even though she folded all those cranes. Radiation poisoning.

Womb-ah womb-ah womb-ah

Oh, my empty womb. I understand it's the size and shape of a pear. But when I think of it, it's hopelessly abstract—more in my head than in my torso. I can only picture a cross-section diagram, done in different shades of red, isolated against the contrasting white of a page. A scarlet light bulb shape, with the pink fallopian tubes attached like alien arms, stretched in crucifixion. My friend Emmy knitted a uterus from a pattern she'd found in a feminist craft book. She showed it to me when I was hanging out with her one evening at her apartment. This was a year before my first pregnancy.

The fallopian tubes were the trickiest part, Emmy said. If you don't stitch them right, she explained, they won't stick out like they're supposed to. See? She tossed it to me and I caught it. A fuzzy pink ball.

It's nice and squishy, I said, and tossed it back to her.

Isn't it? It's my wandering womb. She demonstrated by mov-ing it from one place in her apartment to another—a bouncing path from bookshelf to television top. Television top to back of couch, nestled beside a sock monkey. She also had a pillow that was a stylized vagina made with beige velour and pink satin. I avoided sitting near it.

Blot

After the D&C, the maxi-pad they put on me while I was unconscious lives up to its name. It's thick, long, and fluffy. It strikes me as a relic from another era, a less elegant prototype.

There's only a small spot of blood on it. I notice this as I'm getting dressed, readying myself to go home, still dreamy and slow with receding anesthetic. When I look back to the cot where I'd been lying, I'm surprised to see a large blood stain on the sheet. It's like a Rorschach, and I need to read it. Is it two elephants, walking side by side, one slightly ahead of the other? But no: diagnostic inkblots are symmetrical. This is just a blob. I cover it with a towel.

Rot

No one tells you that after you turn thirty-five, you start aging in dog years. I can see it in my own face, looking into the mirror right now. The wrinkles multiply and deepen. It looks like the skin over my knees is melting. I see the roots of the gray wires that have wandered in among the younger silky strands of hair, little by little. Covering them with dye over and over is like spreading pesticide on a lawn for a few dandelions, but what the hell. I've found that if you pluck out the interlopers, they grow back in to resemble antennae. Their coarseness makes them stand straight up from your scalp. I try not to complain. Compared to what I'll look like at seventy-five, these are my fresh salad days. *When I was green in judgment, cold in blood.* It brings to mind those sad pre-cut salads in a plastic bag, wilting bits of arugula and radicchio that always look like they're two days away from being clotted slime. You must use them up quickly.

After the age of thirty-five, on average a woman becomes 50 percent less fertile. You are born with all the eggs you will ever produce. This seems incredible, inaccurate. Like something that was believed in the seventeenth century, some misogynist bit of hokum. But no, it is true. A man's supply of sperm, like blood, like skin, keeps endlessly renewing itself, refreshed like a Web page.

Yes, but consider the content of the Internet, says Sean. Some of the sperm could be complete losers. Some guys' spunk could be the equivalent of a MySpace page.

Now there's a comfort, I say.

Questionnaire

Was this your first pregnancy? The nurse asks.

No.

She's holding a clipboard, rolling through a series of questions concerning my medical history. High blood pressure?

Strokes? Diabetes? Migraines? Allergies? Any piercings? Capped teeth? She goes quickly, because it's a long list and the information is redundant. I've been over this before.

Do you have any living children?

No.

I'm so sorry, dear. That's very difficult. I hope it works out for you soon.

I don't tell her about the abortion. I want her to keep believing that I'm a good person.

Kitty

I had a dream that we already had a baby—a teeny tiny baby, more like a miniature person, like in *Thumbelina*. But in the dream, the cat had killed it. The dream wasn't about this event, more like the dream was about this event being true. I had an image of the cat, carrying a limp little corpse in its mouth, like a doll. Or a vole. That was not part of the dream. That is the part of the dream that I imagine when I'm awake, because it was missing from the actual dream.

After I come home from the hospital (the actual hospital, this is not a dream I'm telling you about), I look at the cat as she sits beside me on the bed and think, *You are not a baby*. The cat stares back at me, absolute blankness in her melon-green eyes. She yawns and her ears fold backwards, like insect wings. Her mouth a leer of fangs, briefly. She walks over to me and begins to purr, bumping her head against my hand. Sean and I have joked with people about the cat being a child substitute. It's something I need to joke about, often, in order to keep it sounding like shtick. The cat's ears pivot slightly, and then she runs off to the kitchen. Her footpads make thunking sounds on the hardwood floor. I've been overfeeding her again.

When I was a little girl, my family owned a black cat named Minou. I used to dress him up in and push him around in my toy pram. He would struggle as I forced his paws through the sleeves of the little clothes, but once he was fully dressed, he became passive and resigned. My favorite game was to stand at the top of our steep driveway with Minou in the pram and then let it roll down the incline as I chased after it at a short distance, always catching onto the handle just before it reached the road.

Dear

Dear. All the nurses refer to me by this. Like I am a little girl. Like I am simple-minded and adorable. But really: like I am fragile. Such efficient tenderness. Step on the scale, dear. You can put your coat over here, dear. Here's a gown for you, dear. That's right, dear. After it is all done, when I wake from the anesthetic, they will offer me juice and cookies.

The atmosphere is the same as when I had the abortion. The kindest of assembly lines. I remember sitting in a room full of women, all of us waiting to have the same operation. It's a small space, more of a nook than an actual room, and we sit in a circle on wooden chairs. I look at everybody as they look elsewhere. An older Indian lady. A young Asian girl. A woman with blonde hair who looks a lot like me. No one talks. We all wear a uniform. Plush white terry-cloth bathrobes over open-backed cotton gowns. Paper slippers. I keep the white gauzy shower-cap in my pocket. Only one of the women is wearing it already, stretched over her braids. A soap opera is playing at soft volume on a television set, fixed high on a wall. I find it odd that a parenting magazine has found its way into the thick stack of reading material. I suppose some of the women here are parents already and just don't want more. Buncha sluts, I think to myself, but not at all with sincerity. I'm just trying to cheer myself up. Every twenty minutes, a smiling nurse comes and calls someone by her first name. Although the closed unit we're in is referred to as "outpatient surgery," no other kind of surgery besides abortions is performed here. A receptionist had to buzz me in through locked doors.

The baby would have been Sean's. I am five weeks along, which is barely longer than Sean and I have been dating. He has won a prestigious internship with a lab in Europe, one that he's worked for years to obtain, one that can't be deferred. We cannot have a baby now. The decision is mine, and I know it's the correct one. Sean holds my hand and we sit side by side on my green velvet couch. A love seat, ridiculously tiny, like sitting in the backseat of a car. It's the first piece of furniture that I bought with my own money and I will drag it with me everywhere I live. We live: Sean and I will marry a year from now. Somehow, when I told him the news, I'd expected him to be physically disgusted. But his face is gentle, like a man looking at a night sky.

Naming

When I get pregnant again, for the second time, Sean and I celebrate. We make my favorite dinner, pasta puttanesca. Afterwards, we move to the living room with our dishes of ice cream, and Sean gets comfortable by the coffee table with a pen and paper. Although it's our intention to draw up a list of names we want, what we compile is its opposite. We nix the names of ex-boyfriends and ex-girlfriends (even if the associations are positive). Followed by anything that smacks of pretension. And anything overly trendy. Him: anything too hard for girls (Veronica), too soft for boys (Tristan). Me: anything too soft for girls (Charlotte), too hard for boys (Carl). Sean records our non-choices in block letters, writing with his left hand and spooning ice cream with his right. For both of us, certain names have unreasonable yet unshakeable associations. Although our prejudices contradict each other's, we are in agreement that names, in themselves, have the power to bestow flaws and fates:

LIAM — Small penis

ABIGAIL — Cow

ALEXANDER — Jock

JULIE — Joyless bureaucrat

GABRIEL — Dope-smoking underachiever

HANNAH — Gives blow-jobs so people will like her
(Is that true? Doesn't sound like the Hannah I knew.)
(Maybe she just didn't want you to like her.)

ZACHARY — Mealy-mouthed tagalong

BRENDAN — Sneaky coward

MADELINE — Hypochondriac; fake peanut allergy

ANTHONY — Chronic bed-wetter

OLIVIA—The kind of girl who poses for pictures with her toes pointing together
(What do you mean?)
(Like she thinks she's so *whimsical* and *precious*.)

KEVIN—Fatso

NATALIE—Clumsy

CONNOR—Will grow a beard to disguise the fact that he has no chin

MACKENZIE—Self-important tramp; never wears proper bra size

TYLER—Hyperactive

ELIZABETH—Insufferable micromanager

IAN—Republican
(Wait—Ian's a really nice guy. I've known a lot of nice Ians, Sean.)
(Are you kidding? *Ian* is not only a Republican, he's a queer-bashing closet-case Republican. That's who *Ian* is.)

LUCAS—Stupid; hates reading

MICHAEL—Needs a punch in the face

CAITLYN—Bitter backstabber

ANN—Doormat
(I think Ann's kind of cute. You know: Annie. It's sweet.)
(It isn't sweet. She's got body odor. She's a martyr. She's the kind of kid you have to force other kids to play with. Trust me on this one.)

DANIEL—Wimp

JENNIFER—Horse-faced anorexic

We are worse than any schoolyard bullies with these names, with our shouting and laughing. Kids can be so cruel, people always say. Who are we fooling?

There are certain names that we dismiss without pejorative annotation. These are the names with vices that we each secretly find glamorous and strong. Scrapper. Smart-mouthed. Arrogant. Workaholic. Maneater. Ladykiller. Ambitious. Ruthless. Cold. Selfish.

Nameless

I am now eleven weeks pregnant, and Sean and I are at the obstetrician's office for my first ultrasound. In the waiting room, Sean sips his coffee and I talk about preserving the ultrasound image so we can show it to people later. The paper it gets printed on, I understand, degrades quickly, so we should make a photocopy.

In the room with the ultrasound monitor, the technician asks me to shift a little further down on the padded recliner. My feet are in stirrups, and a paper sheet is tented over my knees.

All set? Now, I'll take this and you can reach through and help me guide it in, she says. The wand looks a bit like a microphone, and I think about (just think about) pretending to sing into it (*Feelings! whoa, whoa, whoa*); I realize that I've made this joke before with a vibrator, with the same song. The paper sheet doesn't really cover me, but no matter: I wonder who I'm preserving my modesty for. Sean sits on a high stool, by my side. Maybe all these paper sheets will seem silly in fifty years. Then again, maybe they're a recent feature. My mother, who once worked as an obstetrics nurse, tells me that they used to shave off women's pubic hair and strap their arms down during delivery. I'm not so sure about the strapping the arms down part. My mother's been known to fabricate. Not maliciously and perhaps not even consciously. I suspect her brain splits the difference between the disbelief she anticipates and the truth.

The monitor on my right shows a grainy image, which moves a little as the technician gently pivots the wand. In the center of the screen is a large black kidney bean shape, framed by flecks of gray and white, like static snow on a television. I wait for her to interpret the image. What is the head, what is the body.

Normally, at this point, we would see growth in the fetus. But I'm afraid a fetus hasn't developed. I'm so sorry. I know that's not the news you wanted to hear.

The technician hands me a stack of tissues and in three seconds I need them. After soaking them I stack them and line up the edges, like it's important. I cannot look at her, or my husband as he rubs my back, or the obstetrician who comes in to confirm the bad news. I have let everybody down. My body has lied to everyone. I am my mother's child.

Birdie

Nine weeks into my pregnancy, I talk to my mother over the phone about my fear of miscarriage. So many of my friends have lost babies; I'm aware that it's a possibility.

If you're still barfing and your boobs are sore, those are good signs, she says. I can hear her television on in the background. She likes to watch the silver screen classics movie channel at night while she sorts through grocery store fliers and clips interesting articles from the newspaper.

How far along were you when you miscarried, Mom? I know that she did, at least once. I have it in my mind that she had a stillborn, but I don't trust that archival entry.

My mother tells me that she miscarried in the hospital at five months. A boy baby. I press for details. Did you get to see it?

He looked like a little bird that had fallen from the nest.

This is the most poetic thing my mother has ever said. It is also, to my knowledge, the only poetic thing my mother has ever said. She's sentimental, but that's not the same thing.

If he had lived, I probably wouldn't be here. My brother would have had an older brother and my sister would have had a younger one. Maybe I would have been that little boy. Later on, I look up images of developing fetuses in the book Sean and I have dubbed *What to Expect When You're Expanding*. A baby at five months would be the size of a cantaloupe (the book is fond of fruit comparisons). It must have died sooner.

The Case of the Blighted Ovum

Blighted ovum. It sounds like something you'd encounter on the blasted heath, something that would prowl the moor. But it also sounds right, in that it sounds awful.

Following the ultrasound, the obstetrician explains: with a blighted ovum, although an egg is fertilized and implants, the embryo stops growing. Or it never grows at all. The placenta, however, continues to develop, and continues to secrete hormones.

In other words, my fetus is a phantom. It is a poltergeist, setting objects in motion when there is no one in the room, making malicious mischief.

I think back on the weeks of feeling pregnant, but not being pregnant. Once, after drinking a glass of water, I had to run from the room to vomit. I kept a plastic bag of crystallized ginger in my purse, to nibble on when I felt queasy. I loved the fiery sweet taste, the melting grit of the sugar against my teeth. Even the burble of the coffeemaker in the morning made me feel sick; like a properly cautious mother-to-be, I'd given up caffeine anyway—although I missed it, I needed it, I was so damn tired all the time. I felt dazed, but rather pleased with myself. Sometimes I practiced putting my hand on my lower abdomen in a demure, protective gesture. My secret. I felt like the hostess of a surprise party, hiding behind a couch, poised to spring out and toss glittering confetti.

Old Model

My boyfriend, Brian, is showing me the vintage reproduction anatomy model that he's ordered off the Internet. It's a ten-inch, yellow-white nude woman, reclining on a bed as if sleeping, as if dreaming or perhaps thinking: her expression suggests rhapsody. Her neck arches and her right leg is slightly bent. She is beautiful, with brown wavy hair spread loose over her shoulders, framing her upper body.

The eighteenth-century original was life-size, can you imagine? Brian asks. And she's plastic instead of wax. He taps her miniature thigh, lightly. Brian is a pre-med student with a minor in art history, so he's interested in these things.

But this is the best part, he says. With his index finger and thumb, he lifts away the top layer of her torso, a panel of breasts and belly. Underneath are colored replicas of organs: gray lungs, a red heart, a brown uterus. He lifts each of these out, and places them beside the model on his desk. She looks like one of Jack the Ripper's victims, poor thing.

And look. Brian uncaps the uterus to reveal a tiny beige fetus. She's pregnant!

She's suspiciously pretty, I say, trying to extract the baby. It's fastened in place.

There were lots of models like these. Pretty cadavers. They're called *medical Venuses*.

Yes, a woman like a dug-out canoe, very sexy, I say. Although it is erotic, in a way. Brian and I share a daydream—I'm not sure who communicated it or thought of it first—about him cutting me open on an operating table. Not hurting me, but seeing what other people could never see. A literal intimacy. He will write a poem about it, except that he will be the one on the table, dissected by an unseen hand.

Despite his original plans to become a plastic surgeon, Brian is now in pediatrics. We keep in touch, from time to time. He's married and has twin girls. I saw the photos in a group email.

Secret

At least I know I can get pregnant. Now that I've miscarried, I no longer have to remind myself never to let those words slip to Mom.

How can I tell my Catholic mother that I had an abortion? It is a mortal sin, such willful destruction of God's property. It is too much to tell. Given my mother's tendency for exaggeration, maybe the amount of mercy she already begs God on my behalf will be in appropriate proportion. That's not a cheap shot, by the way.

Nothing

The time that has passed while I was under anesthetic is not like time spent sleeping. It is a pure absence of existence. The film has been cut and thrown away. I have no dreams to serve as souvenirs. I have been somewhere else, somewhere empty.

Of course, that is not the case. I've been put under by the petite anesthesiologist and have lain on a padded table while the obstetrician and nurses tended to my body, reached into me and cleaned me out.

Coming off the anesthetic, I feel euphoric, like I'm being rocked in the bottom of a boat on a lake, warm under a lattice of leaves and clouds. The nurses have likely smoothed the edges with morphine. I'm lying in a cot, now in a different place from the operating area, swaddled in cotton blankets, with curtains drawn around the cot to make a small room. Through a crack in the curtains I can see the nursing station. A stout woman in lavender scrubs is making entries on a computer screen. Sean is standing on one side of my cot, and the obstetrician is standing on the other. Sean has always said that he looks like Santa Claus: maybe, in a hippy-intellectual kind of way.

It's good that you opted to have the D&C, because there was a lot to come out. We got it all, he says. The operation went well. You won't remember any of this conversation, the doctor adds, smiling. He's partly correct. I don't remember any of it until Sean tells me what he said hours later, when we're at home.

Trying

I'm drunk on my own hormones. For a change, Sean adds. Oh, ha haa, I say, putting a touch of British into the last syllable. But he's right. There were some bad old days. Not that Sean was there for them: he just heard. That was back when we both would have considered each other un-dateable, living rather loose and large. Now we're married and trying for a baby. We're ready this time. I've been off and on the pill for almost twenty years, but now I'm off. My last pack of pills is housed in the medicine cabinet, each blister pocket empty.

I'm having a feng shui consultation with my friend Celine. She walks around our apartment, making comments and offering suggestions as I take notes on a pink spiral pad that I bought at the dollar store for this very occasion.

You should really think about moving the bed so that your feet don't face the door. That's a classic feng shui no-no. It means death. Bad for baby-making. Celine squats to look under the bed and laughs as she nearly loses her balance, teetering on her high-heeled boots. And also, she says, you need to clear out all the stuff you've got stashed under here so the *chi* can circulate. What are those—old magazines? Get rid of them. Clutter's bad. Blocks energy.

Celine suggests that we buy some plants for in the bedroom and also for the other rooms in the apartment.

Live things are good! But make sure you water them. Keep them healthy. Nothing like a bunch of shriveled plants to put the kibosh on fertility, Celine says. She then tells me about a recent consult she did for another woman trying to conceive.

So I was walking through her house, and one of the first things I see, right off, is that she has a rotting pomegranate, right smack dab in the middle of her Children and Creativity area. Really! How long has that been there, I'm thinking. Talk about a *symbol.*

Huh, I say. But I wonder: Who eats pomegranates? Not that I'm doubting Celine's story.

Pomegranate

I have eaten a whole pomegranate once in my life. My mother brought a few home from the supermarket, moved by some rare whim. She placed one on a plate in front of me at the kitchen table and I examined it, running my hands over its shiny red hide, tauter than an apple's, gathered at the top in points like a tiny crown. Give it here, my mother said, and slit the fruit with a paring knife. She let me bend open the cut seam, which produced a faintly hollow cracking noise, and I marveled at the exposed seeds. I thought they looked like ruby teeth, clustered together in some luxuriously eccentric profusion. My mother tucked a linen dishcloth around my neck. It's messy, she said.

This was years before I read about Persephone. Her marriage and bargain with death. Her bereft mother. In the mythology book I won years later, as a prize for proficiency in Classics, there are charcoal illustrations of Persephone emerging from the underworld, her arms extending upwards from a hole in the ground, reaching towards a weeping Demeter, and of the pomegranate, with the fatal seeds extracted and piled to one side.

(I ate all the seeds of the pomegranate, sucking each one white, a drop's worth of juice at a time. It's not that they were sweet, but that they were so beautiful and so many.)

morning of confused purposes

where to go from here
waking from tangled ambitions
from tangled sheets and restless hours
memories of loving innocence
oh this breathed into life from clay we are made of

well the cards came alive yesterday
imagine a bases loaded homerun
and this from the pitcher himself
oh the good carpenter we had
shaving his bat to a shining perfection

what was I dreaming
I wish I could tell you
and tell you the names of those
hundreds of friends
who came in and out of my life
that was in the old days
why hello again richard and tom
ray and julian good buddies

and sweet old dream dates
oh a taste of salt there with the honey
you have a right to your privacy
and I wish you only the best
may the years treat you with loving care

well this is as far as I can go
only to say that this noon is overcast
and there is an impudence of pink asters
and a straggle of goldenrod
beneath my study window

lines for an old friend

at four oclock the birds in the garden
attend to their psalms
it is that sort of a becoming
beginning with a consecrated hour

overcast perhaps

this weekend on saturday
we will go to the farmers market

what to find there
all that our far flung neighbors
have drawn from this rich black earth
our central illinois legacy

what am I saying
all that is alive this day
should lift us up

should hurl us into a heaven
beyond our needs beyond
everything that we could ask for

hold me kindly in your thoughts dear
as I fashion these words for you

[The Birds Begun at Four o'clock —]

This is not the dark wood, or the midway
            ha-ha stumbled over. The birds
   eke out a song over the din of leaf
            blowers.
    Into the
           roar they cry
    domain, display their best
            sex-me plumage.   Because I am not
   burdened by indecision, there are no
        Eleusinian mysteries — I'll always
go to the underworld rather than
   undergo this world much further.

        No, nothing dramatic — I mean
  all this in gesture — the dark,
       tall, and lordly — that's who I
fob myself off for. All these

orioles can give it up because when I
    untie my heel's strap and
        reveal myself in the glory
of my shabby bedroom — such a
     cacophony of secondary sexual characteristics.
        Later I will rise to Spring's
   oboe tones, and reborn, shower all who
call love to the unlistening air, with
     kisses of the most exquisite insincerity.

I Do Not Fear Hats

They've come into my house
and behaved commendably.

They believe in God.

Once in a photograph I saw
a soldier take his off before

kissing his wife. (At least,
I assumed it was his wife.)

Once all men wore hats and

you knew where they stood
on the great chain of being: a

top hat or bowler, red fez or pith, a
hard hat, Panama, fool's cap, fedora

and the kind with the small

propeller. I don't
know them all.

When the Final Trumpet has sounded and the Vials
poured out, God will appear in the best hat of all:
ermine (I'm guessing) with spotlights that shine

into even Saint Augustine's soul.

Two years before, I'll start a hat sect.
I'll be the Grand Hat Master.
Angels will love me

though now

I'm aroused by the nurse's cap.

Balloon and Ribbon

Why would you hold back
a balloon if its sole wish was to rise?
mother asked. *To keep,*
I said. She untied the ribbon to prove
what her worldly eyes swore,
it zigged like a bee,
and for whatever reason
a man caught it
from the 13th floor roof —
his body like an anxiety
reversing, dropping dull
and flat on Zoloft,
the creeping hum of rubber
volleying against wind
missing by inches
the streetlight hooked
like an endearing question.

Dani Neff, *The Lonely Red Balloon*, acrylic painting

Speaking to the sun

—the title you asked me to pencil in
above the picture you had drawn, your head laid
across your forearm for ten minutes or more, intent
on depicting a garden richer even
than the one we had worked in all morning.

Done entirely in orange crayon, with sunflowers,
and a gardener and the sun itself
all the same size and color, all smiling to each other
like neighbors chatting over a low fence.

Each drawn with a certain weight—
sunbeams and flower stalks in the same strokes
as those you used to frame the one human
you've allowed to stand among all your work.

Even the balloon around the words
you have her speaking, now that you ring
my title with your fat orange crayon—
all the same weight, the same thickness, the same,
the lines that forever link the speaker
to her thoughts of one moment
on possibly an August morning.

You hold it all out, at arm's length, and regard
the alchemical moment that I'm forever
spelling my way toward and never quite conjuring,
and your garden, your art, becomes the place
I wish we lived, where every element
is perfect, is evident, where words
can never be thrown away and we're happy
to carry the banners of our every thought
over our head for all to see.

Loft

A morning barn in March is winter's chapel,
Cold-choired with pews of hay
High as rafters. Pigeons court and gabble
In mourning coats tattered and gray

As city streets. Through pinpricks the light
Splinters the planks, broken stars that glow
Blue as carbuncles in morning's night.
Bales mount the apse of shadow

Toward a frozen pediment of sun and wings
Under this restless tremolo of roost and coo
I can't follow, the birds calling
What sounds like *go figure it out,*

Go figure it out, in a Canadian accent.
In cones of sunlight a few dust motes drift,
Flutter, then zig in a lazy ascent
Toward the goal of air's lift,

To get up and out. My breath, too, tufted
Bird born in this frozen nest, aspires
To rafters then disappears, lifted
Like the longing that always fires —

Oh please — another day. Far above the floor
Stained with leavings, something opens
Along my ribs where the whole shawl of air
Ripples like liquid toward the glassless attic pane,

Blood and ink cooling toward the same stop.
I'll stay below on the shit-stippled ground —

Dust and kids can climb where the day erupts
Along pillars of rye grass, crackling sheaves bound

With twine. Only let me walk home under purple ghosts
Of maples splashed across the snow like maps
Of their own fall, trunks stabbed with steel to tap
Their ichor, pails tipped like heads of curious dogs.

Manly Johnson, photograph

Apples to Oranges

> This is not supposed to be a virtuoso trick
> —*Milton Babbitt*

But it *is* supposed to be a type of challenge,
like a grope toward a rhyme for orange

or other fancy trope, Elizabethan-style whore-binge
of sound for poets who rise — or plunge —

into the whacked-out word-party hardcore grunge
that puts them squarely on the poor (lunatic) fringe

of love distress. I've been there: one more inch
and you know you're over the top or edge,

so lost and bent and glazed you couldn't gum porridge
let alone manage the simplest rhyme or extend your range

of possibility, everything suddenly, as they say, *apples and oranges*,
as if comparison itself were just bacillus dead in the dour syringes

of commerce, Whitman's grass so much Astro Turf, as if Stonehenge
were only a *coupla big rocks*. The stale falange

of the literal everywhere prosecutes its sour revenge,
and for what? A few sunbaths on the rug of the present, when awe inches

toward us like summer; times we spiced the blancmange
of rules and regs with gin and rebellion and felt no twinge

of regret — like that basement Ethiopian joint, where your *injera*
and my kneeling declarations oiled the door hinge

of pleasure's gate, fresh as a wedge of peeled orange.

Conversion

The snowy parts stay visible longest.
I can see the white slope by the red light of the Ponderosa's
welcome sign.

I think of it as a bargain: in return I could believe
they'd meet me at a gate, fifty years from now—

                                      Then there is what I like
about Bibles: their front page, the family tree mirroring,
but so much shorter than, always,
Genesis' lists of begats.

I think about God saying please.
I am, He says. All those wives, and their names changing—
They wave. Soft where the snow pixelates them, each reddened by the
       thrill of naming.

Mark Weiss, photograph

Frozen Letter

Leaving something alone becomes a friendly gesture:
                                        the red snapper bare
on the sidewalk for two months three winters ago,
and even the cats didn't want it. It's how I met my neighbor. We'd talk

about it, his arm his, still, but in its stillness
belonging to his future,

which is to say his death from cancer.
                                Our flirtation endured

nerves numbing, a tumor pressing his shoulder the way a thumb
would press, or a pair of suspenders.

I Could Call It Holy

Morning's another black-birded affair.
The dull weather maintains itself,

thunder bruising clouds to ashen blue.
If I want to see darkness, it's there.

Shadows in nature—true,
these I've never understood.

I want to ask,
Which question do I want to ask? but wonder:

would that simply raise more questions?

Whether these matters trouble
is no question: they do.

But I'd rather witness day with
unspoken awareness of Something, somewhere

that *knows* I have no clue.
Holds all of it together.

The Loon's Cry Folds

into its own world   disappears
tremolo diver   within the ever-changing origami of the sea

sea we walked away from   our feet, jeremiah anchors
sink into wet sand   as if in remembrance

during the breeding season   male territorial songs
hurtle   each desperate call knifes

into scar tissue   opens/ closes/ opens
the moonstone door   of desire

if only we had not lapsed   in eden's liquidity
what wild magenta laughter   might scaffold us toward god

Reflections

The distinction between past, present and future
is only a stubbornly persistent illusion
—*Albert Einstein*

The wasps that had taken over the kitchen
cabinets, the cellar entrance, did they hum, *Go away*?

Or, *Come*? As my son and I spread
your ashes in the creek nearby, we rang your

knotted rope of bells. Mother, Father—
What memory of you did their tongues dispense?

The dead leave us with reflections. Father's eyes cede
the elusive color of water. Mother's lips

coathanger my mouth. The document found
in a cranny of the inherited desk, with farmhand

ciphers—number of ewes, number of lambs—
has started to disintegrate, ink blurring

into ink. Each time I pull the glass knob
to lower the desk lid, I feel Mother's hand inside mine.

Semen is the tributary through which we pass,
womb the bridge we cling to. Until we ladder down

into the laddered world. Who lifts the pen
onto this sheet of paper? Father, did you hand me

the words I woke up with—*Cast a line into
the river, the river makes room for it.*

Crossing the Cahaba River on a Fallen Tree, My Brother Breaks His Arm

I don't remember Silas falling,
though he did and I was there
so must have seen. I don't remember
his landing or lying on a bed of creekstones,
though he must have. I remember
the water oak's dirt-caked roots
spidering into the air, this giant
ripped free from its tethers,
and the cold breaking of the spring river
around my fist, then around each finger
spread wide, testing—the same water
that years later pressed against me
and a woman I thought I would marry
as we held on in the Atlantic Ocean,
the waves seeming to part around us
as around one body but secretly slipping
through the small unavoidable spaces between us.

The leaves must have gone yellow already,
paper-dry, dying. He must have cried out:
a wounded sound that echoed over running water,
even my brother who fears nothing.
How old would he have been then? My father,
younger than I am today, carried
him home through Gillespie's pasture—
it must have felt a hundred miles.
Some memories are true because the body says so.
The hospital air was cold, the light a pale green.
I would have been hungry—I was always
yearning for something. I did not know
the questions my parents were asked
when the x-ray found some healed past
injury, a transparent gray smear
where clean white bone separated, grew back.

They must have explained we didn't have
a telephone. Even thirty years ago
we were not ordinary. I mean this as a good thing.
Was that the year my father had a beard?
Were my mother's hands still dirty
from the morning's weeding?
Did nurses eye a hole in the favorite
faded Dodgers T-shirt I wore everywhere
and wonder, meaning well? The body
can't know every detail. I remember
the ride home: a green pen from the glove box,
a skull-and-crossbones on my brother's cast,
parents complaining over our heads,
the gearshift rattling fiercely at our knees.

Manly Johnson, photograph

Buddies

Three of us are paddling kayaks on a lazy river, a hot day.
We like it that you leave a car at put-in, another at take-out,
can't turn back along the way. Middle age
is like the place on the river where we are right now,
a slow bend, carp sunning in the shallows, mud
baking on shore. Our brains so many eggs, the sun
on dirty water, brown from the runoff of towns upstream.

Larry is snapping hopeless pictures of a heron
fishing motionless in the shallows, a tiny dot on his LCD.
Suddenly that bird gives up, flies low
directly overhead, as if smiling for Larry's camera.
"There you go, man," Chaz says, *"there you go!"* And soon

we're talking about luck like this, moments of apparent grace,
and using phrases we can use to agree with anything:
There you go, man, there you go!

"I can't paddle next weekend, too busy with the dating service!"
There you go, man, there you go!
"Since my layoff at the plant, I'm a lot less depressed about work."
There you go, man, there you go!

To be this agreeable is to fish in easy waters
and fly from point to point hardly lifting a wing,
guided by instincts so true they seem to be smiling.
It's merely our turn on the planet.
We paddle slowly and the brown river moves.

Larry is divorced and going out again;
Chaz and I are not, and not. Advice from the two of us
is best left in the distant cave of the 1970s.

"I don't think I should wait around and let my ex just…"
Why would ya?
"I should shop around before I commit to a woman who…"
Why wouldn't ya?

"My little brother thinks I should date that girl
in my welding class at the technical school."
There you go, man, there you go!

"Fuck buddies," Chaz intones.

His son tells him kids say now they're fuck buddies.
Just a weekly romp, then back to the daily wars.
The concept is strange to us, in no cave, no
old vault we have the combination for,
and not in the silver maples along the shoreline,
turning their light leaves in wind, almost against the rules.

Maybe *that's* what you need, one of us says,
and after the silence after the laughter,
a pair of eagles lifts off from a pair of trees
and every sunning carp knows to flip into the brown river and hide.

Mary Hargrove, photograph

Stem Cell

After Bartolo De Fredi's "The Creation of Eve" (1356)

While he slept—head pillowed
by a length of arm, naked on moss
and the softest grass—she began
to grow inside the marrow
of his curved rib, inside the flesh
that settles just above the hip, a bit
of blood fresh from the final chamber.
Out of this her head appeared, then
the reach of humerus and radius, clavicle's
bridge, and last the blush and promise
of muscle's pink shadow. When her hips
cleared his side, she stepped away, her wonder
balanced by femur, her gaze upon the trees,
the glistening shapes of fruit, upon the flower
of her vulva from which more fruit would fall.
Have you ever watched from a boat
as catfish spawn? In this garden, chaos
and fury shaped our love, but out of that shape
something more: the voice of God,
or the simple sound of wind
among turning leaves.

Somnambulance

All the sleepers who rise from their bodies and peer
down at the sheets and blankets that cover them
leave a cast of their slumbering, shadows where their heads
pushed deep into pillows. In what way will we know
if we have loved God? Like Lazarus, the dead are wrapped
in sheets, buried in night-clothes. The living enter sleep
the same way. In the morning, may we rise and pray
when we hear the voice of the one we love. May the stench
of death be washed from our mouths. May Christ not weep
for what awaits, whether grief or simply some long awaited sleep.

John Milisenda, *Vivienne*, photograph

DAVID THACKER

from *Fetus Dreams*

for Liesel, in utero

1. Blue

While mother backstroked laps
in steady rhythm to buoy
the weight my presence causes,

lolled by her effort, I dreamed:
like water in a cloud, adrift
blind among murmurs, a boat

lost, I was nowhere —
an amoeba awash in microscope light,

illuminated like halogen. I expected
to see iris fibrils looming

magnified across the sidereal, the infinite
pool of a pupil. I saw nothing
but sedate motion: dense ripples — wakes

descending like cold air or a propagated
sadness — my body, beautiful
wadded blanket I was swaddled in.

I remember her breathing — each
inhale's up-strum — and could hear
careering blood, could sense,

in my dream, the beat of her flaps
on the water's surface and, propulsion

through more inevitable dolor,
shoves to keep us moving.

2. Sunlight

This far along there isn't much
        separation from air. So it shouldn't
                surprise I pressed prenatal palms
        against the inner wall
of my weighty balloon, pushed,

        legs propped
                like a car's jack, until
        belly tissue, vessels constricted,
                bruised in my hands. Forgive me, mother;

        your flesh shone
like cheekskin around a flashlight
or a faceless jack-o-lantern.
                As I stretched the soft rind
                        farther, gossamer membrane,
                Chinese paper lantern aloft,

        aurora borealis burst
like purple myrtle down your womb,
        which I held long
                and painfully, I'm sure,

        in my hands. I only
                wanted to be light
                deep in the sun,
                rushing out.

The Imaginary Colors of an Imaginary Brain Scan

The hemispheres of my brain still miscommunicate, even
on Olanzapine, making colors into more
than they are, as if red were really the ultimate

blood. And orange was those sweet evenings
we spent peeling tangerines
down to their taste of late afternoon,

and yellow was the sun dancing
over your kitchen wall making it look like light
could breathe the theater of shadows

in unimaginable colors, and blue
was that color we love when mystery seems
protected from us, somehow, like twinkling stars.

And lapis lazuli and ruby
are the colors of the cross,
but gold seeping through green

is the color we got when it was autumn,
and we were falling, the way
night is falling

fast, the way every poem is Icarus
falling, through the sound of the word, "Olanzapine,"

back through summer towards the beginning
of spring, when we were looking forward
to evenings full of dark green
moonlight,

and white was the color of the morning,
when the world hurt
our eyes with heavy sunlight pressing
us from all directions.

We felt like we were full of grace,
and that lavender scent
of wildflowers. The flowers mixed
and danced with the bronze

wind, and the breeze still
carried the wildness, faithful,
as always, to both sides of the
black-misted mirror.

Then the whooshing of the metro's sound,
here in my mind, on the corner of St. Denis
and Mont-Royal, fuses with the Green Line,

C Train, of the Boston subway, when it rattles
above ground, and the maroon incandescence
of windblown paper bags

fuses with the glaucous call of a seagull
echoing through the Massachusetts seaside weather,
and all the colors are there, rainbowing yet clear,

in an oil-slicked rain-puddle,
on both sides of my brain's hemispheres.

Panic

When the elevator went down, he heard the voices behind him, but the other passengers in the elevator—a doctor in a white coat, and some kind of girl in boots—their voices drowned out the others. "When are you going for lunch?" the doctor was saying. "You can't work through the whole afternoon."

The yellow people, who had been with him all morning, didn't like elevator rides, and they'd be waiting for him at the bottom. They usually were friendly, and the elevator made them nervous.

"I have a couple more hours in the library," the girl with boots said. The toes of her boots grew longer, as he stared at them, so he looked up at the numbers, with the red light flashing behind, until one of the numbers smiled at him, and he had to look away. The toe of her boot was moving across the floor of the elevator like a snake.

❊ ❊ ❊

In the interview room, Dr. Mukhapattee's face was pale wood-colored, a soft brown like his big eyes. He spoke softly, which Jacob appreciated. The doctor's face was surrounded by a yellow light, which made Jacob hopeful.

He nodded and told the doctor he was going back to practicing his guitar.

"Good," the doctor told him. The doctor seemed tired, and Jacob smelled paint on him. "I smell paint," he said.

"I'm having my apartment painted," Dr. Mukhapattee said. Jacob sensed Dr. Mukhapattee's tiredness, and his kind feelings for a woman, someone young with joyful black hair.

❊ ❊ ❊

The long summer grass is gray in the humidity, which rises off it. The hills are empty except for the grass, that swishes against itself, the hills roll down like water, gray, the grass talking in the afternoon sun.

❖ ❖ ❖

"What do you think about the reality of love?" Jacob asked the doctor.

Dr. Mukhapattee said, "Why?"

"Do you love me, Dr. Mukhapattee?"

"Yes," Dr. Mukhapattee said. "Everybody loves you. We all love you, and we don't know what to do."

❖ ❖ ❖

Months later, Jacob finds himself in the Metropolitan Hospital locked ward. The interior of the hospital common room is drowning in fluorescent light. The walls are beige, and metal occurs here and there like a staple holding up a stage set. If he looks at the walls long enough, they begin to peel back, and he can see the dark spaces behind. The infinite galaxies, spread like humming insects, that go back and back beyond the door to the laundry room, if you open it. The two wooden locked doors with the chrome handles across them, locked to keep him inside, when they open reveal the places outside, and today, when the visitors came screaming at each other in Spanish, the outside rolled in across the floor like green shouts. *Mira. Mira.* The vegetation of Puerto Rico, big leaves, lush, they brought with them. He had to go back to his room, and sit on his bed, to avoid getting his feet dirtied in the green.

❖ ❖ ❖

That afternoon months before, he had gone to the Institute library on the eleventh floor, to see if the girl with the boots was there. She had a large red line around her face, pulsing with shadows. She typed on a laptop. The yellow people hadn't caught up with him from the elevator; a bell dinged as it shut. "Do you work here?" he asked the girl. "I mean, do you work?"

"Yes," she said. Smiling.

"I'm in a clinical trial," he told the girl. "Some outpatient thing they're doing downstairs."

❖ ❖ ❖

A few nights after Jacob is committed to Metropolitan, Sam the RN comes to chat with him. He is a nice man, with a long face, and sideburns. He laughs easily. He asks questions about the voices. Jacob says he doesn't have any. "What would you describe your anxiety level as?" Sam says. "I'm not going to patronize you. You're smart. On a scale of one to ten, with ten being you can't stand it."

Jacob listens, nodding, smiling, seeking out the holes in the floor. There aren't any, right now, which means that Sam is not lying to him.

"You want something to sleep?" Sam says.

"No," Jacob tells him. He understands that Sam is sympathetic. Somewhere in his life, he's been in a dark place himself.

"You want to talk about how you came in here?" Sam says.

"It doesn't make any difference," Jacob says. "Today is not the day I came in." He sees that Sam is writing with a Bic pen. "Today is a Bic," he says. "When I came in, it was Pilot. I prefer Bic."

Sam nods. "Right," he says. "You know I work here five nights, and if you want anything, you come to ask me. Cigarettes, or whatever you want."

"Thank you," Jacob says.

"This time here is a transition," Sam says. "Until you get straightened out."

"Dante is lost in the woods."

"In the middle of the journey of my life," Sam paraphrases, "I wandered, lost in the woods. I know that from college. *The Divine Comedy*."

The red faces, the warners, erupt behind Sam's ear. Behind his head. They warn Jacob by becoming his thoughts. He waves his hands to erase Sam's words in the air, which are dangerous, like knives that will cut the walls open. He hurries back to his room.

✤ ✤ ✤

He is clear on what happened at Stanford. He had a girl-friend, who may have been sent by the others, but he thinks, most of the time, she was not. Before the nature of the true energies of the universe was revealed to him, she was a blond girl who listened while he played the guitar. She wrote poems about her unhappiness. She wrote stories about him playing the guitar, about his body. He cannot think about it now, but they spent time naked in his bed together, and he remembers his orgasms, huge blasting waves he could not control. Possible happiness. Nights of whispering, when her face seemed to glow in the dark. Her breasts. She came from Berkeley. Her father was a surgeon, and later Jacob thought that meant she might be like him, a cutter.

He went to his classes, wrote to his mother, and got B's. His mother wrote that she was all right being alone, she was seeing Frank. The tone of her letters was chipper. He got an A in a course called World Civilizations. The professor invited him to come to his house with other students, and he brought his girlfriend, and they drank wine with dinner.

Being a freshman wasn't bad, he wrote to his mother. His roommate, who was studying Eastern religions, bought some pot laced with something else. This roommate, who was from New Mexico, tried to get him to smoke it, but he demurred. His roommate tossed up his hands mockingly. "I respect that," he said. "It's crazy, but I respect it. You might want to go into government work."

At the end of the spring break, his girlfriend, Melody, said she thought she was pregnant. He remembers sitting on the quad, watching the students lacing in and out of the pillars of a covered arcade, thinking that life left trails behind it, even after the body disappeared. He could see them weaving. Melody said she almost wanted the baby, but she decided to get an abortion. He told her she was wrong. They fought. He told her the baby was from God. "Before you were in the belly, I knew you," he said, quoting Jeremiah. She went home for the weekend, and when she came back, the baby was gone.

He was stricken, as if he'd killed the baby with his own hands. He stopped going to classes. He stayed in his room, sitting on his bed, praying without letting anyone know he was praying. His roommate, thinking to help, gave him some pot, and as soon as it hit his bloodstream, he went into some other universe. The walls were unstable. The wind and water and human voices twisted into a semblance of speech he did not know. The objects around him, even his own hands, twisted like snakes when he stared at them. He knew he had fallen off some edge, and he was alone with it.

This is how it was reconstructed later, when he was back in New York, having dropped out of Stanford.

He was eighteen years old. He had committed a terrible error. Wrath was going to destroy him. The people were sending him messages all the time. If he sat, the voices nattered behind him. The faces of the doctors he was sent to by his mother morphed into the faces of animals. One was a dog, another a devil. A third was a camel. He learned to sit quietly, smile and agree. He was afraid to say what he saw, because the people became enraged when you told anyone about them. He lived with panic.

✻ ✻ ✻

That afternoon at the Institute library, the girl with the boots, who was named Esther, finished her typing and dropped it off with her boss, the doctor in the lab coat. He said to Jacob, "How's it going?" with his eyes like snow. A Nord. He understood, and had no pity. "How's it going," Jacob said to him. The girl took him out for a sandwich at the Greek diner on 167th Street. He told her about the secret lives of eggs. The beginnings that linger coiled in eggs, which is why he wouldn't eat them. They took the subway to the park next to St. John the Divine to look at the peacocks. The birds came up and he fed them the rest of his sandwich, and they picked at the ground, where the sandwich had fallen. He said he used to play the guitar.

✻ ✻ ✻

At Stanford, the professor talked about the Greeks, whom he already knew about, and the gods of the Romans as well. The cults of Mithra, Cybele, the other gods he has come to know personally when they speak to him about certain happenings. Events in which he is participating.

✻ ✻ ✻

After they met, Esther helped him. She walked along the street with him, and because his shoe sole was flapping open, and he was alert for invasions, people stared at them. Because he had trouble speaking directly, he stammered. A man passing by looked at him curiously, and then more curiously at her. She said he looked like her brother, who had died. He told her he liked to play the guitar, and she gave him a guitar that had been her brother's. He played, with odd chords that ran easily and then became dissonant in the middle of a song. The fingers taken over, he felt the song go somewhere else where it wanted to go. She gave him the guitar to keep, and he was happy to have it. The next time he came to visit, the guitar was slung over his shoulder like a club, the strings dangling broken, the back stove in. Eventually he forgot it somewhere.

❊ ❊ ❊

At Metropolitan Hospital, Sam the RN comes to chat with him again. He asks if Jacob can sleep. "What about something to help you stay relaxed. You want that?" As he talks, the floor tiles develop huge holes in them. Sam is lying. He's come for the shot of Haldol the doctor ordered for him.

"No, thank you," Jacob says.

"Jake, we got to," Sam says. Jacob hits Sam right below his mouth. Four orderlies put him into seclusion. The rest of the week, he can't have any visitors. He sits by himself on the floor in the corner. They gave him the shot of Haldol anyway; three held him down, and Sam gave him the shot. "I'm all right," Sam said to one of the other orderlies. The first two days in seclusion he just sleeps, except when Sam or someone else comes to lead him to the bathroom.

❊ ❊ ❊

Esther comes to visit, but the head nurse tells her to come back on Saturday. When she comes on Saturday she walks through the common room doors with red streamers around her, and the vegetation is swept back in waves. She brings Mars bars and Hershey bars.

"Your hospital is better," Jacob tells Esther when they're eating the candy bars. "Isn't it."

❖ ❖ ❖

The toe of one of his father's shoes had come unglued, so his bare foot showed. He left it like that, so the shoes were asymmetrical. The forces he sometimes picked up on streets, when he was walking behind people, were confused by asymmetry. Sometimes he wore the shoes on the wrong feet, to repel these forces streaming around him.

He wore his father's tuxedo, and his dress shoes, which he got out of the dark closet with the smell of mothballs. He wore them to visit the clinic.

"Afternoon, Jacob," the nurse said. "You look like an ad for a Rolex."

"It's because I have to watch it," he said. She laughed. Behind her, the shadows were forming faces. He laughed because she laughed, and the shadows dispersed while he was laughing.

"Where is Dr. Mukhapattee?" he said.

"He's on a different rotation. He's gone to a different service."

When he sat down with the woman researcher, who had dangerous earrings, like points of blame, she wanted him to see the new doctor about increasing his medication.

"We can raise the dose. I think you need a little more."

"I'm fine," he said.

He was trying not to stammer, and he knew that more of the med would make his tongue even thicker. Yesterday, he'd wanted to drool all afternoon, because he was tired of swallowing all that saliva. Just now, for half an hour, he went into the bathroom at the clinic and drooled into the toilet, until the men using the urinals outside, who were speaking Spanish, said they wanted to go to a festival, and he knew it was a code word. Festival, fester, part of what was eating his brain.

He ran out of the bathroom and frightened a woman waiting on a bench in the hall. "Slow down, motherfucker," she said.

❖ ❖ ❖

His mother's boyfriend Frank plays the piano in a bar on 50th Street. He's short and wears a black vest. He reminds Esther of someone from a story by Damon Runyon. The floating world. She

49

feels uneasy around him, because he plays the piano for gangsters. Strip clubs. He stays at Jacob's mother's apartment on Park Avenue, bought by the father with the tuxedo.

❊ ❊ ❊

When Jacob is in Metropolitan, Frank throws him a birthday party in the hospital. "Put your glad rags on," he says when he invites Esther. He brings a cake with candles that the head nurse says Jacob can light, but has to blow right out. They eat the cake. By that time, the top of the cake is showing Jacob messages in the pale yellow icing. Words from the yellow people, warning him about the head nurse. After his visitors leave, she'll tell him it's time for his weekly shot. He hardens his muscles, to repel the injection. After six weeks, now he finds that he can't control the drooling at all. His feet slap on the floor when he walks. He can pay attention to the programs on television; they're about a dog, and a talk show with a beautiful woman who tells about her divorce. The television rarely gives him advice, anymore. But one afternoon it does: "Wait in the bathroom," it says. "We can talk to you in the water." He runs the water in the sink, a gray steel basin that shows a blurry outline of his face. The water contains a soft song about Hiawatha. A melody. He runs the water until the nurse comes to stop him. "Come on now," the nurse says. "Back with everyone else, where we can see you."

❊ ❊ ❊

Jacob's mother still owns the apartment on Park Avenue. She says to Esther, "When his father was alive, Jacob wasn't like this."

Frank says, "There was an aunt with problems, back in Tennessee."

His mother wears a dark dress made of velvet, a deep neckline. She's living with the old furniture. The Park Avenue apartment has the decay of something not changed for twenty years, once grand, now smelling of smoke and a lack of housekeeping. Dark interiors, with grand things, not cleaned.

"I had Jacob when I was thirty-five," his mother says.

Frank smokes a cigar, standing behind her. He met Jacob's mother when she came to the club, with her husband. He is devoted. "The aunt. My husband's sister," his mother says in her southern accent. "I never knew her, but she had to go away."

Esther wonders why his mother seems so calm amid this chaos. The apartment, overlooking the Avenue, that the management must be dying to get them out of. The doorman who has known Jacob since childhood, and nods hello as he comes and goes, with his ragged clothing, his symbolic outfits, his father's neckties, the wardrobe he has depleted, week by week, for the last five years. "I buy him clothes," his mother says, "and he loses them."

The girl imagines sweaters all over the city, new, light blue sweaters, gray, tasteful. His mother doesn't seem sad that he loses them, or angry, either.

※　※　※

On her sofa, she listened to Jacob talk for hours, when she was exhausted and he wouldn't go home. He talked in poems, in codes, in images that stood for something else. Talk of light and shadows, she thought. Like no talk she'd heard before, not even in the poems in classes she'd taken. The speech that was other speech.

※　※　※

"Well, I don't know," his mother said to Esther. "He was just fine until he went to college."

Esther would later tell her boss that she was surprised how uninvolved Jacob's mother seemed about everything. She didn't even visit him in the hospital. Her boss, who had just spilled coffee on his lab coat, told her that it was a cluster of genes. "It's a whole complex," he said. "We don't have enough studies. But if he's got enough of a load, she's got part of a load. She's going to be unusual herself."

※　※　※

Esther sat in the Park Avenue living room, waiting for Jacob to finish his bath. In a while they would go walking across town, where passersby would stare at them on the street. They'd go to the club where Frank was playing. Esther waited in a chair of exquisite French brocade that smelled of cigarette smoke. The presence of Jacob's dead father had been spilling out of numerous closets as Jacob had been dressing himself over the months. Umbrellas, trench coats from Burberry's, handmade shoes, several tuxedoes, suits made in England.

"His father's family moved to Memphis," Jacob's mother said. "That was where I met him." She seemed to take everything as equally probable. Esther, whose life was full of financial and emotional uncertainties, marveled again at how Jacob's mother, with this extensive strangeness around her, found nothing strange at all.

"They were from Philadelphia," his mother said. "They came before the American Revolution."

Jacob emerged wearing his pajama bottoms. He slowly put on his father's Burberry raincoat, and tugged on one battered dress shoe. "Wear socks, at least," his mother told him.

He got up off the brocaded settee with its French gilding and returned after several minutes with a pair of huge white athletic socks, that he put on slowly, as if he were doing it for the first time.

"Do you need money?" his mother said. "I don't have any."

"I have some," Esther said.

They changed plans. They went to the movies on 96th Street, but had to leave right after it started, because the words rolling across the screen, appearing and disappearing, were too specific. They told him to get out of the theater. Something bad could happen in the dark, with Esther. He would hurt her like he hurt the other blond girl, whose name he couldn't remember, except when he heard the word meaning something else.

❊　❊　❊

Melody sits on his bed in his dorm, and tells him she's missed her period. "I got the test, and I got the red line."

He waits for her to finish. "I'll get it taken care of," she says. "You don't even have to think about it. But you could give me a couple hundred dollars. I owe my mother."

I've killed her, Jacob thinks. *She doesn't show it yet, but it's going to come to her slowly.* He is filled with a self-disgust so intense that he goes into the men's bathroom and vomits. When he looks at himself in the long mirror over the sinks, there are, for the first time, moving lines around his eyes like hundreds of small automobiles of different colors.

❖ ❖ ❖

One night he came home to the Park Avenue apartment with a broken front tooth and a red, swollen eye. His mother told him to stop riding on the subway. Especially late at night.

❖ ❖ ❖

When Jacob brings Esther up to his mother's apartment, the doorman looks at him strangely, because the doorman is new and he's heard about Jacob.

"His father's family was six generations in the mountains in Tennessee," his mother says. "Jacob never went there. But originally, they were Quaker, in Philadelphia. They had to leave, because of some problem with business. I never paid attention." Her fingernails are scarlet. Esther feels more dislocated by Jacob's mother today than she has previously.

❖ ❖ ❖

On the night that the final game of the World Series is played in Yankee Stadium, Jacob walks through Central Park. The bushes are hiding people, sometimes real, and sometimes the voices. A woman under a streetlight asks him if he wants a good time, until he gets up closer, and she says, "Never mind, honey." He sees that she is a woman and a man. At the edge of the lake, he takes off his father's shoes, and the tuxedo, and his shirt, and drops them in the path. The streetlights, like old gaslights, cast cones in the dark. He flings away his belt, and kicks off his pants, his boxer shorts. It's a good night for swimming. The fountain's shut off, but the lake water glitters red and purple. A pair of men pass him, and watch him, walking naked. When they're past, Jacob hears laughter like the barks of dogs. The sounds carve like knives across the back of his head. The air. The yellow people haven't shown up since sunset. He stops at the edge of the water, in the rushes, and wades in where some plastic bottles and other trash float. A food wrapper, translucent, rattles against the shore, bright white. He covers his ears, to see if the sound of his own legs splashing in the water will echo less. The water reaches his waist, he ducks his head under, getting a noseful. Under water, the voices change, the roar grows louder, as if a train is bearing down on him. A train, coming right through the water, and up into his head.

He swims, floundering, up as far as the bridge. Strikes his foot against something sharp in the water, a bright blue pain. When he stops, gasping, hanging on to the stone piling of the bridge, trying to get his breath, the yellow voice winds down the pylon, and enters his left hand.

When the men come to get him out of the water, he runs across the grass, and when they catch him, and put a silver plastic sheet around him, he swings at one, until the solid one, who doesn't talk to him as if he's a fool, hits him in the windpipe.

"Why are you out here without any clothes on?" the young one says. "You looking for business, or what?"

"No, he ain't," the solid one says. "He's a section eight."

Jacob's throat has a huge buzzing crater in it.

"You ain't supposed to be out without clothes on. Where's your clothes?"

"This is the way God made me," Jacob says, struggling until they pin his arms behind him.

"Amen to that," the solid man says. "Call it in. We need another heat blanket."

"Come on, nature boy," the smaller man says. His face streams with a thousand red tears that lift off his cheeks as if the wind is blowing them. Except even Jacob knows there isn't any wind.

"What is it with these guys?" the man driving the car says. Reading the laptop on the car's dashboard. "They like the spring breezes, or what?"

"This is the way I was born," Jacob says. The police officer, the one without the blanket, who tackled him in front of the statue of Alice in Wonderland, keeps holding his arm as they drive.

"Come on, Alice," he says. "You got family somewhere, or did they already give up on you?"

❊ ❊ ❊

His second stay at Metropolitan Hospital, the regular doctor has been rotated off the service, and Jacob does not know the young resident who appears to evaluate him. A short, dark young man. Huge brown eyes that are rotting in the middle. Ambitious.

"What's up?" the resident says, when they're alone at the table in the common room on the ninth floor. The resident leans his chubby cheek on his fist. He's tired.

"I'm hungry," Jacob says. "I'm hungry with a hunger no food can fill."

The ambitious resident types on his laptop. "You want a meal? They can order one."

"They can write my name on the side of the potatoes," Jacob says. "And everyone will know how important I am."

The ambitious resident types more. He tells Jacob he needs to have his foot sutured, they'll go back down to the surgical ER. The resident's looking for something to make important, that he can tell people about. He wants to make Jacob something important, but he doesn't think he can.

"My foot isn't clean," Jacob says. "Can you see?" He laughs.

* * *

The wind blows over the grass, on the hills of Tennessee. He watches the grass bend, in a long sweep, as the wind touches it. Red, and blue, and coral and green.

* * *

He'd looked through the ashtrays to find butts big enough to smoke, and found two. Since his last shot of Haldol, his hands had been shaking so much that he had trouble getting the flame to the end of the butt. He pushed his hands together, as carefully as he could, but it was hard to make them touch, the black end of the bent butt and the match's flame.

Now that he was back in Metropolitan, the shots came twice a week, and he had trouble dressing himself. His hands shook so badly he needed to ask someone to hold the match, or else he burnt his fingers. He inhaled to keep the voices away, with the whoosh of his breath. The girl Esther came to visit him after he called her. She brought some books and candy, mostly Mars bars and Reese's Peanut Butter Cups. He was always hungry for sugar.

One afternoon he was having a slow dressing day, and he was naked, standing looking out the window. He'd finished his shower a while ago. The city rooftops outside the window were pumping slowly up and down, moving across the sky whenever he let his eye rest on them. Saints were hiding, ready to manifest themselves in those buildings. Sometimes the brilliant light of a saint sparked off one of them, as the sun moved. He knew the nurses were going to come in and tell him to get dressed, because the doors were open. But when he heard someone at the door, and turned, it was Esther, with a paper bag in one hand.

She saw his body, pale, the fine muscled torso, the genitals nestled in blond hair between his legs. His buttock, the jut of his hip. He was beautiful. It surprised her.

She turned and fled before either of them had a chance to speak. He got dressed slowly. There had been a red shine around her. Even now, in the heaving room, with the points of the steel beds standing for rules of behavior, as reminders.

Later when he sat across from her in the common room, she gave him the cigarettes, the Mars bars in the paper bag. He stared at them after she set them on the table between them. She said, "I'm sorry. I didn't realize you weren't ready. They said to go find you."

He said, "What was that, Esther? Was that Aphrodite?"

She didn't answer. He felt an enormous sadness with her, heavy in the stomach. She herself ate one of the Mars bars, and it made her smile, and underneath it all, a new fear. She had been thrown backwards by what she saw. Her face was white.

"What did you do today?" she said.

He didn't answer, because he couldn't remember anything. They sat for a while and didn't talk. "Okay," she said finally. "I'll be going."

When she left, he said, "Goodbye, Melody."

By the time she'd gotten to the end of the hall, where the elevators were, he'd turned back to the common room, where the TV was showing a game show. He sat to watch. He didn't think about Esther. By nine o'clock he would have his meds and be in bed. Sleep came easily.

❖ ❖ ❖

He sees the hills with the grass whispering, that he has never seen. The long, rolling reach of the sun, across the surface of the hills like water. He comes again to the mountains of Tennessee. The fair sweet wind, with a thousand voices that carry him along with their promise that when he opens his eyes, the world will be solid. That every shoe and toothbrush and grain of salt will stay in its place, silent, and the life will be gone from it. The duty of the earth, its heart, will be where he wants it to be.

Mark Weiss, photograph

The Arrival

The Arrival, L.A.

The bus is smoking as it pulls into the slot between a Grey-
hound and a Trailways. Not like Camels, mind you. Fumes. Lili
smells dust and petrol. The haul had been long and dirty with a
big-time logjam in a snowstorm in the panhandle. Texas wasn't
used to that kind of snow, not like New York, not like the East.
On the highway outside of Amarillo the bus sat still for three days.
Twelve of them in a vibrating tube, the engine on for warmth.
There was a strong smell of urine and all that comes with that,
from the stuffed toilet. Finally, they got off the bus to pee, hiding
under sixteen-wheelers, crouched and pretending they were invisible.

Lili was the cheerful helper on the bus in Texas. She kept
busy picking up trash, walking down the line of cars looking for
food for the crying three-year-old passenger. There was a cute guy
in a Chevy two cars behind. He winked at Lili the first time she
went past in the snow with no boots. The next day he went walking with her down the row of cars. She was asking for milk at that
point. Then the State Police showed up with milk and food for the
kid, and some for them. They got the cars plowed out and moving
by the third day. People were shuttled by tractor to local houses
overnight, but Lili and the other eleven passengers remained on
the bus. It was a kind of home.

* * *

The bus pulls into the downtown L.A. terminal. Lili picks
up her suitcase and climbs down the stairs. Three days late for
arrival. She sees them immediately, standing by the ticket window, two very short people. A man with red hair, in a suit, and a
woman with blond hair, also in a suit, with a skirt.

They don't spot her, don't know what she looks like. She has the jump on them, a few seconds to scope it out. Before. Then she says, "I'm Lili."

The Goodbye, N.Y.

Six days earlier Lili had carried her suitcase down the stairs bumping, banging into all those travelers, buses burping announcements, "9:45 to Poughkeepsie, Gate 31, leaving in five minutes"; "10:15 to Los Angeles, Gate 28." Lili had waited on line. There was a sound of distant humming   She was going, going. She heard before she saw her.

"Lili, Lili!"

Lili did not turn to see. She knew it was her mother.

". . . . .not going. No. You are not. Changed my mind. Come home. Now."

Lili shook no.

"A mistake. *Ich kennisht.* Can't do it. You need to stay."

Lili followed the line of travelers as it trailed out the door to the loud drumming of bus in gear.

"No, Ma. No. Please. I have to go. Sorry. Sorry."

Lili got on the bus and put the suitcase on a seat next to her.

The mother was standing looking at the window. She was mumbling, her mouth moving. Lili changed seats to the other side of the bus. Gone.

The Social Workers, N.Y.

At school, la di da, all those bouncy smart high school girls, giggle, giggle, where were the boys, oh yes, all girls. At school the guidance counselor had said, "Is something wrong, my dear?" The principal had called her in. The social welfare ladies, they'd come to save her, do good, do good, they were asking for surrender. Lay her down, your mother, lay her down over here. Sell her out, they said. She is sick. Tell us, they smiled, tell us how it is with her, just you and her. Don't you want to come away? With us?

No, no, no.

The Bath, N.Y.

At night, in Brooklyn. Lili always returned late. It was four subways from the Forty-Second Street Library, at midnight when it closed. Four subways and the walk in the dark, stars, buildings, her hood up. Up the stairs and in the door and the sound, the sound of mumbling. Lili went to her room. Snow piled up near the broken windows. Rocks, they threw rocks, the neighbors, kids. Who were they? Lili's mother was yelling about metal plates on her brain and the computers reading her mind. The neighbors threw rocks. "Shut up, you witch," they said. And worse. Lili put down her schoolbooks on the dresser. She Scotch-taped the plastic bags over the broken windows. She took off her peacoat and the sweat-shirt with the hood. And the pleated skirt with the pin holding it closed, like a kilt, like in Scotland. She went to the bathroom and shut the door. She ran hot, hot water in the bath and stepped in. She put her fingers deep into her ears and slowly lowered her head under the water, covering all but her nose. She floated.

The Momser

Lili had lived in L.A. once before. Before New York, when she was a little girl. She and her mom. In a tiny bungalow behind another house across the street from her mother's friends Gitle and Moishe. It was a time of palm trees and ocean and oranges. Trips to Yosemite where Gitle got a cinder in her eye from that fireworks extravaganza on Half Dome. To the Golden Gate Bridge, wake me up in the middle of the night, I want to see it, please, please. The motorboat on Lake Tahoe; oh, oh, my hat, and the boat turns around and goes back and there it is, bobbing on the wake, thank you.

Gitle and Moishe, so short like her mom. All of them short and the lisping sound of *tsuris* and *krechts* and *gottanyu* and *kasha* and *tsimis*. Brisket and borsht, tea with sugar cubes between front teeth. Saturday night at Sonya's, they were all there, Sonya and Schmuel and Gitle and Rifka and Bernie and Isaac. So many of them. The women erupting into piercing soprano, *Tumbala, Tumbala, Tumbala laika*, and then an oh-so-sexy alto, *Ba Mir Bist Du Shain*. Her mom with those tiny ankles and the platform shoes. Gitle with her thick legs and a butt like a barrel. Sonya with her head plumped down into her neck, her chest, her breast.

They said, "She looks just like her papa, Pierre, that little one."

"No, she's the mother. Just like Germaine with that dark hair, but the dimple, maybe his."

"A *shmendrik*, how could he leave such a little cabbage?"

"A skirt chaser. A *momser*. I don't care, so he's a big *macher*, him and his articles in the *Forward*. Don't give me he had to go back to save humanity. Save his *knaedlach* is more like it."

Lili's mom stood up and grabbed Rifka and began humming the Miserloo. Da da da da. Arms around shoulders, one arm in the air, legs crossing forward and back. The snake of the dance around the dining room table, pumpernickel and pickles, through the hall, and into the living room. Everyone joining in. Lili clapped.

The Arrival II, L.A.

Moishe smiles, at the bus station when she arrives from New York. Lili remembers his smile from back then, from before what came after. Moishe smiles and takes Lili's face in his hands. The hands with the needle-holes scarred from the years at the machine. He kisses her on both cheeks. She is taller by far. She is sixteen, he is fifty-seven.

Gitle says, "What has she done to you? You are so thin. *Shrechlich, mommela.*"

Moishe says, "Sha. Not now."

Gitle says, "Hurry. A party. Let's go home and get you into clothes. Nice clothes. You have nice clothes? Something. We are late."

Lili reviews the contents of her suitcase. The suitcase that lived under her mother's bed all that time, packed with letters to her mother from Pierre, from her sister in Paris, "Dear Germaine, missing you . . ."

In the suitcase Lili finds a suit her mother made for her, a copy of the suits she sewed at the shop. Herringbone, with a tight skirt and a box jacket. "Like Jackie's," her mother crowed. "In *Vogue* it was." Lili wears that suit. It itches; it's wool and is too warm. She is now in L.A.

Gitle and Moishe live in a wedge of a house over by the high school. A house for small people, set behind a building of apartments. They had it made out of an old garage. Moishe manages the building, and they are part owners, a mitzvah for two immigrants from the shtetl. Moishe struts. "Twenty-seven units," he tells Lili. "Takes a diplomat. Everyone a story. This one, he can't pay the rent, he had back surgery and is out of work. That one needs the money to buy his beer. He says, next week. A bunch of *ganiffs*. Feh."

The house with low ceilings, living room, two sections of oatmeal couch over here and over there. The kitchen with a new long counter, high as Gitle's breasts when she stands and cuts, cuts a little melon, a little pineapple, to bring to the party. There are two tiny bedrooms, small as closets. Lili's with a studio couch and desk. They name it her room. The couch opens into a slim bed. Her feet will hang over the end, like dead fish. Lili thinks, Better than a bath, better than a coffin. Better than snow for a pillow. A whirring. Mom in her bed, talking, talking. Lili dresses for the party.

She enters the party wearing the wool suit. Upstairs one flight through an arched door she sees Swedish spare furniture, clean. She sees people, strangers. "This is David, you remember David? And this is his wife, Betty. It's a birthday party for Betty's mother." Lili was told on the ride over, a ride in a clean new Chevy. She rode in the back to the birthday party.

❖ ❖ ❖

Once Lili's mom made a party for her birthday. She was eight. There was a cake from Babka with candles, and her best friend Ella came over from the apartment next door. There was a present, wrapped, from Lili's mom. When Lili opened it she saw a portable record player and a record of showtunes played by an orchestra. Lili thanked her mother and put on the record. She didn't mean to, but she began to cry. She couldn't stop. Her mom pretended not to notice, and they ate cake. Afterwards, they sang the song and Lili blew out the candles. She made a wish but wouldn't tell.

❖ ❖ ❖

At the party at David's—he is the son of Gitle and Moishe— at that party Lili meets the family. There are David and Betty, married five years already, Betty's mother and father, Betty's sister Sue, and several of Betty's aunts and uncles and their kids. Sue tells Lili that she doesn't seem like a Lili. Maybe more like a Lisa. Lili is very tired. She wants to go to bed. Any bed. The bus trip had been so long. She sits on the clean couch and practices posture. She had learned in speech class back in New York. How to sit like a lady. How to stand like a lady. Her mother had told her to stop slouching or she would grow up with a hunch like their neighbor, Mrs. Applebaum. Lili sits in her herringbone wool suit and breathes. She waits to be brought back to Gitle and Moishe's apartment so she can go to bed on that little couch that opens up.

A Day in L.A.

In the morning Lili carefully makes the bed back into a couch. She folds all the covers and sheets. She dresses in a skirt and blouse and blue canvas sneakers from last summer and walks the five blocks to the high school. It is a big brick building on Olympic. She finds the office and gives the woman her records from her school in New York. The woman—she is quite nice, smiles a lot and smells of coconut—she brings Lili to a classroom. Lili tells the woman that she wants to be called Lisa.

It is an English class, first period. The teacher, an older woman, tells Lisa to come stand in front of the class. "Boys and girls, we have a new student and we need to welcome her. This is Lisa, and she is joining us from all the way cross-country, from New York. Lisa, why don't you sit here for now and we will find you a permanent seat when class is over."

Lisa sits in a chair next to the teacher's desk. She is facing the class. All those eyes looking, they are watching her. She stares out the window and sees palm trees and sun. There are no clouds. She waits for the class to end.

The Boy

In the hallway between classes there is a boy, he looks like Elvis with a big wave of dark hair curling down his forehead. "Hey, New Yorky," he says. "Why'd you move out here?"

Lisa answers, "I came to live with friends of my mom. My mom got sick."

"Sick?"

"Yeah." Lisa stops talking.

The boy says, "I'm Stu. Wanna ride home? I've got my car."

Lisa laughs. "No one drives in New York. I can't believe kids drive here."

Stu meets her after school and drives her around before he brings her home. He has a convertible, and Lisa lays her head back on the seat and looks up at the sky. She has gotten one wish.

The Letter

*Dear Mom. How are you? I miss you terribly. Gitle and Moishe are
nice to me, but I miss home. Are you okay? Please, please write. Tell me
everything. Love, Lili*

At night she dreams of her mother. In one dream her mother
is screaming and pulling out her own hair. In another her mother
opens the door to Lili's bedroom, and Lili sees that the top of her
head has been shaved. There is an egg-shaped lump of scalp. Lili's
mother says, "They hit me with an umbrella, those *mishugenahs*.
On the subway. Crazy. Craziness. Lili, come with me, you'll help
me. You should tell them to stop."

One time, it wasn't a dream, Lili's mother looked her in the
face and said, "You will write the President."

Lili said, "No."

"Lili," her mother said. "You will write the President. Tell
him. Tell him what they are doing to me."

Lili sat down and wrote. In longhand.

*Mr. President. Please help my mother. They are listening to her
brain. There are computers. She doesn't know what to do.*

Lili put the letter in an envelope with a stamp and walked it
down to the mailbox near the train. Like writing to Santa. They
didn't believe in Santa, not at her house.

The Police Come, L.A.

It is on a Thursday. Lisa has walked to school and been
driven home by Stu six times already. She knows she has to tell
Stu she can't keep going out with him. She has made some new
friends, girls, and they have invited her to rush their sorority.
They told her Stu was bad news. No one likes him, they said. A
loser. Lisa likes Stu. He is sweet and kind. She sees the kids
stop talking when he comes up to them. She knows what she has
to do, and fast. She wants to be in the sorority, to sit at the table
with those girls at lunch. There is a guy who has asked her for her
number. He is on the football team.

That Thursday, while she is writing a note to Stu, telling him,
the teacher calls her name right then, in math class. "Lisa. You
need to go down to the office." Lisa walks out of the room and

down the hall. A noise like wind when there is no wind. Down the stairs, into the office. She sees the uniform, a policeman. And Moishe. Short Moishe sitting in the Principal's office. Moishe and his accent when he says, "Lili." Did he say *bubbalah*? Did he say *tyreh*? Did he use all that sound, the sound of a spigot open and the whooshing greenhorn whistling of the dead people?

What did they want from her? They want her to know. It will be a relief, they say. "Your mother is in the hospital. They will help her get better."

Lisa thinks, You stupid people. What do you know? You want me to be happy they locked her up? You want me to thank you for coming to my new school and all those kids hearing? Seeing me with a policeman. With this short Jew from Poland. I hate you. I hate you.

Lisa does not say a word.

❊ ❊ ❊

Lisa sends underwear to her mother in the hospital in New York. She buys them with money Gitle and Moishe give her each week for allowance. She doesn't understand allowance. In New York she had a job, she had her own money. Here she takes her three dollars a week, saves it up, and buys a few pens and underpants for her mother. She puts these things in a manila envelope and mails the package to her mother at an address in Queens that the policeman gave Moishe on a piece of paper. Lisa keeps the paper in her suitcase. With the picture of her mother in a bathing suit on the beach in Brighton. The one with her smiling and holding her hand above her eyes to block the sun.

The Sorority, L.A.

Lisa gets asked to join the sorority. There is a meeting in the attic of Cheryl's house. Cheryl lives in a large white house with a big lawn and a metal fence keeping it all in. The twenty girls are in the attic giggling. Lisa sees that she is one of two or three girls with dark hair, the others are blond. Long blond hair; some wear it in a ponytail. Cheryl is explaining the rules of the club. At one point all the pledges, Lisa is a pledge, go wait downstairs in Cheryl's room. One by one they are invited back to the attic for the initiation ceremony. Or maybe it's for the selection. Lisa waits nervously with the other girls. As each one returns from the attic they refuse to tell the others what happened. Lisa picks at her nails. She pulls her long hair up into a bun and then lets it fall down. She means to smile.

When her turn comes Lisa joins the girls in the attic. They ask her to sit on a chair in the middle of a circle. Each girl asks Lisa one question and gives her one task. Jenny says, "Tell us about the first time you did it with a guy." Lisa is stunned. She hasn't. But she did come close with Lenny back in New York. Should she say she did it? Is it cool to have sex here in L.A.? Or should she act shocked?

She jokes, "Well, there was this guy in New York I was with for a while, and he was pressuring me. One night we were at his apartment and his parents were gone, but it was the weirdest thing. Every time we started to get into something heavy the lights flickered. I mean off and on. After about five times we both got so spooked we got out of there and went bowling."

Lisa can't tell if she gave the right answer.

Jenny says, "So you're a virgin?"

Lisa says, "Well, I didn't say that."

Jenny says, "Cagey."

Cheryl says, "You've had your question, Jenny. Let's move on."

Lisa answers questions about her ideal guy, her idea of friendship, her most courageous act. She does not talk about her mother. She does not talk about the bath and the rocks and the time she stayed in her closet for a whole night with her fingers in her ears.

After all the girls ask their questions, Cheryl says, "Okay, the final rite of passage is you need to undress and show us your naked body, to prove that you will obey our every command from now until thirty days from now. We are your masters. You are our slave. Do you understand?"

Lisa shakes her head. She is not sure here.

Cheryl says, "Strip now."

Lisa starts to pull off her shoes and socks. The girls sit silently. She begins unbuttoning her blouse, but at the third button she stops. "I don't think I want to get undressed."

Cheryl says, "No? Are you sure, Lisa? This could mean the end of your chance to belong to Tri Sigma. Think carefully."

Lisa sits still, her hand on the third button. She wants to cry. She doesn't. She remembers a time at Gristede's on Broadway when a kid who worked there had gone into the back to find a package of lima beans for her mother. While he was gone Lisa's mother said, "Give him this fifty cents. A tip, for when he comes back. I'm running to Babka for a challah."

Lisa said, "No. That's his job. People don't tip here, Ma. I don't want to give him the money."

Lisa's mother said, "You will give him the money."

When the boy returned with the beans, Lisa said, "My mother wants me to give you this." She threw the coins on the counter and ran out of the store without the limas.

✻ ✻ ✻

Lisa says quietly, "I don't want to undress." She puts her shoes and socks back on. No one moves.

Finally, as Lisa rises to leave the room, Cheryl jumps up and yells, "Welcome to Tri Sigma, new initiate! You made the cut."

Lisa thinks, They are making fun of me.

Jenny says, "It's so gross when those girls actually start taking off their shirts. God, remember when Mary Alice got all the way down to her undies last year? I thought I'd puke."

Someone says, "Who wants to see a naked girl? Yuk."

Lisa laughs. "Yeah," she says. "Yeah."

The Weekend

On the weekend Lisa goes on a ride with Gitle and Moishe to Sonya's house. Lisa sits in the back seat of the clean Chevy. She has brought a book, *Jane Eyre*, and reads it the whole way. Past Mexican outdoor markets, past green parks with sprinklers and yelling kids, past a Mercedes-Benz dealership, and banks reflecting cars from their glass façades.

Moishe says, "Tonight, dinner at David's. Betty's sister comes."

Lisa says, "Oh." She was at the part of the book where Jane has saved Rochester from a fire in his bedroom and realizes she is in love.

"A *mishuga* teenager, boy crazy. And stupid, an empty *kop*. Nonsense, she talks."

Gitle interrupts, "Moishe, *genuch*—enough. Sue is young yet. Not everyone is an Einstein."

Lisa likes Sue. She lives in the Valley with her parents, in a ranch house with plastic on the couch so Pookie the dog won't make it dirty. Sue vacuums every day for her mother. Her mother has card parties and likes the house clean. Sue makes BLT sandwiches and tuna melts, American food like on TV. Lisa loves the times she gets to visit Sue's house. She has stayed overnight twice and sleeps in one of the twin beds in Sue's room. They talk until late and Sue's mom keeps coming in and telling them to go to sleep.

Lisa always wanted a sister. Sue is just her age. She is tall and thin and has a boyfriend named Bobby. They have done it, lots of times. Sue says she loves sex. She laughs, "It's like candy. Yum." They do it everywhere and anywhere. "Like rabbits," Sue says. Lisa isn't sure what rabbits do. They don't have rabbits in New York. Sue says she and Bobby have done it in a park up against a wall. Lisa listens and tries not to gasp. She is surprised. She has done everything but. With Lenny. He has promised to come out for the summer, to get a job and rent a room somewhere, to be with her. Lisa thinks they will do it then. In New York she had other things on her mind.

Saturday night at David's, Sue is there. Lisa and Sue take a walk after dinner around Olympic and Robertson. Past the Jewish deli and the drycleaners. Past the butcher with the Arabic writing on his sign. Past the art gallery with a painting of a big Buick convertible in neon colors. Sue asks Lisa if she wants to smoke some grass. Bobby got some for them. Lisa says, "Sure." She isn't sure. In L.A. she has become greedy, like a pirate stashing booty. A fearlessness, or something else.

Sue steps into an alley and lights the thin cigarette with a match. She pulls hard and tells Lisa to hold her breath as long as she can. Lisa has smoked Marlboros since last year. She sucks the grass deeply and tries to keep it in. She coughs. It hurts. With cigarettes she likes to ring the smoke, puff it out her mouth and draw it in her nose. This is harder. After her third try she stops. She feels something and laughs. Sue is watching her and looks silly. Lisa snorts.

Back at David's apartment Lisa is goofy with goodwill. She offers to do the dishes. She tells Betty her new rug is great. She teases Moishe about his being the smartest, yes, a leader of men.

When Sue catches her eye they both fold into giggles. Moishe says, "Silliness." David says, "Ah, the young." When they leave for home Lisa says, "I am so glad you're my friend, Sue," and Sue hugs her tightly.

The Inquisition

On Tuesday Gitle tells Lisa she can't go to Sue's on Friday because they are driving to visit a cousin in San Diego. Lisa begs to go to Sue's. Bobby is bringing his friend Richard over and they were going to double date.

Gitle says, "Not this time. I want you should come with us."

Lisa writes a letter to Lenny. She writes, "I hate Gitle. She is old and mean." She doesn't tell him about the date with Richard. When she leaves for school on Wednesday morning she props the letter against the lamp in her room to remind her to stamp and mail it later.

Wednesday after school Lisa walks home. When she enters the little house she finds Sonya and Schmuel sitting at the table with Gitle and Moishe. Lisa says hello.

Sonya says, "Come sit." Lisa puts down her books and takes a chair. There is a smell of watch-out.

Lisa says, "My mother?"

Moishe says, "No."

Sonya says, "It's you, Lisa. You. Disappointed we are, and surprised. Such words from a girl who should only feel gratitude. Did she teach you to be thankful? Your mother. Did she not?"

Lisa is quiet. She does not understand.

Schmuel says, "Did you write these things in your letter?" He points to Lisa's letter to Lenny, out of its envelope, on the table. Lisa is confused. How did the letter get here? What was in the letter?

Lisa says, "I don't understand."

Sonya says, "Did you write, 'I hate her'? About this giving woman, this saint sitting here? This woman who told your poor mother to send you. Who has taken you into her home."

Lisa looks at Gitle. She is staring at the table. Lisa says, "I don't remember if I said that. Did I say that?"

Moishe says, "Lisa. Do not lie."

Lisa does not move. She sits and waits. The phone rings, and Moishe gets up. He calls Lisa over. "It's for you. Make it fast."

Sue is calling about Friday night. Lisa is crying. Sue doesn't understand. She says, "Bobby and I will drive down. Hold on, we'll be there soon."

Lisa returns to the table and waits. She waits for Sue to come.

Dinner

Lisa helps make dinner at Gitle and Moishe's. There is chicken, boiled. And potatoes, boiled. And a salad. Lisa cuts the vegetables for salad. Gitle makes the dressing. She pours lemon juice and olive oil onto the salad and then sprinkles salt and garlic powder. Lisa eats the leftover salad in the big bowl every night after the compote dessert. After the coffee is poured. Lisa takes the bowl and eats every leaf of iceberg lettuce, every cucumber slice dripping in that dressing. Gitles says to Moishe, "You see. You see how she loves my salad. *Is geschmacht*, no? It's good."

Gitle is in the kitchen. She says to Moishe, "A shame, a horror, what Germaine did to her. Crazy she was, but a child without a childhood . . . . It's no wonder Lisa doesn't know her head from her *tuchis*."

Lisa hears. She thinks, My mother was right. Lisa is not sure of the truth here. Gitle is in the kitchen whispering. How will Lisa know? She wants to know. Maybe she should write the President.

The Letter II

Dear Mom, How are you doing now? Are they going to let you go home soon? Do you get outside at all? Did you get the last package I sent? Please write and let me know. I am okay. Sometimes I miss home a lot. And I miss you. Love, Lili

The Sorority

Lisa has been pledging Tri Sigma for three weeks. The sorority sisters run into her in the halls or in the courtyard at school and give her specific tasks. Jenny is in charge of clothing. She tells Lisa, "Wear a plaid skirt tomorrow, and then find a different plaid blouse and wear them together." One time she told Lisa to wear her shirt inside out with the tags showing. She had her wear one knee sock and one short sock. Lisa doesn't mind. Everyone can tell when kids are pledging.

Cheryl has directed Lisa to ask out the football captain. His name is Chuck. He is tall and blond and wears his hair long. It falls into his light blue eyes. Chuck was dating Cheryl until a month ago. Now he hangs around with the cheerleaders.

Lisa likes John. He is on the football team, too. He is the boy who runs back for the ball, so thin and fast on the field. John is in her math class and is very shy. Once John asked Lisa for her phone number and said he was going to call to see if she would help him study for the math test. He never did, but Lisa is still hoping. John always comes over to her desk and says hi. He asks if she has a hard time with the homework. She says yes every time, in case it is hard for him.

Lisa does not want to ask out Chuck for Tri Sigma. Chuck doesn't even say hello, and he doesn't know her name. Lisa cannot imagine going up to him. And even if she did, what about John? He would hear about it and misunderstand. Lisa doesn't do it.

Cheryl says, "Lisa, I haven't heard any little birdies talking about you and Chuck. Come on, little sister, time is a-passin.'" Lisa doesn't answer.

On Monday she calls Sue. "I don't want to ask the guy out."

"So don't, for Christ's sake."

"But then what? Then I won't be in Tri Sigma. And I've already gone through the worst of it."

"What do you want to do it for anyway? It's stupid."

"I don't know. I think it's cool. I've never been in a club. Maybe I can be in Homecoming or something. Like in the movies."

"Lisa, it's stupid. Dump 'em."

On Tuesday Jenny gives Lisa an umbrella. Black. She tells her to walk across the lunch yard with it open and sit under it while she eats her lunch. Lisa does. As she is sitting there she sees Chuck walk out with two cheerleaders, Sally and Kitty. Lisa doesn't move. After they walk by Lisa closes the umbrella. She sees Jenny head her way. Lisa says, "Okay, I've had enough. I don't want to do this anymore."

Jenny says, "For heaven's sake. You're almost there. Next weekend is the big dance. Don't be a killjoy, Lisa."

Lisa is quiet. Then she says, "I think this isn't for me," and walks back into the school.

When Lisa gets home that day there is a letter from her mother. It is in a blue envelope with handwriting that looks unfamiliar, shaky and unsure. Lisa opens the letter. It is short. Here is what it says:

Dear Lili—I am doing not so bad. I received your packages. Thank you. Another week they will keep me here at least. The Daitches visit me. They will take me to their apartment. Maybe they can find me my own soon. Please send a few dollars if you have money for cigarettes. Love Mom

Lisa, Lili. Lili from the old world. The *alte cockers* and the trembling walk down the boardwalk in Coney Island. "It should be a sunny day, *vey iz mir*, always it is cold here, *nu*? *Kalt mit die vind. Shrechlach.* Lili, be a good girl, *zeeskite*, and *brengt meine* glasses, I should read the *tzeitung* here on this bench in the sun. *A bissle* warm. *A kleyne bissele. Meine tyreh* Lili, the flower that smells so sweet."

Lisa said goodbye to Lili at the entrance to L.A. High. Really before. She became Lisa and rewound the story to the beginning. It began on the bus ride and continued at the palm trees. Lisa at Grauman's Chinese. Lisa at Disneyland, and Universal Studio. Lisa the Homecoming Queen. No, not that.

Homecoming

It is the big game. Lisa is on the short list. Nominated for Homecoming Queen and then the test. Here she comes, Miss America, Bert Parks, Miss California. Lisa walks into the auditorium, head balancing an invisible book, her back straight. Yes, I am so pleased. Yes, honored to be among you. My most courageous moment? No problem. This is my moment. Or was it when I wrote the President? No. When I got on the bus. No, in the bath, in the bath. Shall I show you the fingers in my ears? I can't hear you. No.

Lisa is a Princess, not a Queen. It is a matter of balance. There is a black girl who is Queen. Lisa and an Asian girl and a blond cheerleader are the court. Red, white and blue.

Lisa brings Bobby to the dance. When Sue lends him out, Bob says, "Why, sure." And when he walks Lisa up to the stage, she pretends it is Lenny holding her hand. Tonight they would do it, if he were here.

She wouldn't have left New York. No, not on her own. Each day at school and the library and that job. All those subways, changing trains, trains stopping between stations, men's hands and did he touch me there? Each day, the papers and tests, and Lili, your grades are slipping. "Why?" they asked. She did not say. She did not say this or that. Each morning emerging from the bath cold, skin like a view of the Alps, puckers of ridges. Each day the black skirt, a black high-neck shirt, and onto the subway before the sun. Each day a smile, a big smile, and all that fun. At school. And the girls.

She would never have left the up and down of it. In those tight black pants, all bone, and who knew? Nedicks, Ray's Pizza, the cafeteria and then those girls.

It was her mother who did it, who called L.A. Germaine asked for a home, and Lili heard. She heard her mother on the phone, in the lateness of the night and the snow falling. "Gitle, I will send the child. *Ich hott nich koyich.* No more strength."

Who could have told her such things as this? Things almost forgotten, like palm trees and sun and ocean waves. Boys in cars and up the Pacific Coast Highway to Malibu, the name like chocolate. Lisa, Lisa, suck me down the tunnel of love and spit me out here, over here. "I will return here," she must have known. "Yes."

Regret

Lisa wakes in the dark of the night. She has been yelling in her sleep; she heard it. She was screaming, "No. No." Her mouth open in a howl, like a tunnel, a cave. A deep, dark place. The dream always the same of her mother walking, walking, pulling her hair out and walking. Her mother screaming, "Take off the plates." In the dream a man is pressing buttons on a big machine and her mother is attached to the machine by wires. Her arms and legs jerk when the man presses the buttons. The man is in the shadow. He looks like Lisa's father in the picture she has, the one where he's in uniform wearing a grin. The *momser*.

Lisa wakes in the night and thinks of her mother in the hospital all alone. She pictures her mother stretched on a table, tied down, and pumped with electricity. She has seen a movie about crazy people. They are shocked, with wires to the head. Her mother's nightmare. Lisa wakes and wonders if her mother was telling her the truth and the others are lying. The truth about who's in charge, and who is crazy.

In New York Lisa had a friend named Paula. Paula lived in Far Rockaway. When Lisa went to sleep over at Paula's, Lisa's mother said, "Paula is not a good friend to you. I know some things. Paula's mother and father want to take you away from me. They want another little girl so be careful when you go to Paula's. I am telling you this for your own good."

Lisa worried when she visited Paula. Paula's mother was very nice to her and made Lisa's favorite food when she came over. Paula's parents owned a clothing store, and they gave Lisa a skirt once. She was afraid to take it home with her. She thought, Maybe they are trying to steal me away. I must be careful. Lisa said no when Paula invited her to visit after that. It did not seem wise.

Lisa's mother told her that her friends at school like Patty and Sarah and Rhoda, she said, "Lili, they don't really like you, they are just using you. Don't be an idiot. Use your *kop*, your head, be careful."

Lisa wakes up in the night in L.A. On the short couch-bed at Gitle and Moishe's. She sits up in bed and says out loud, "Mommy, I'm sorry. I'm sorry. I'm sorry." Lisa rocks in the bed and cries, "I'm so sorry I left you." Lisa says, "Mommy, I couldn't help it. Couldn't help it."

Lisa pictures her mother's face outside the window of the bus. She lifts her hand to wave goodbye. She never said goodbye.

The Arrival III

Lili gets off the bus in L.A. and sees the two short people. She thinks, They are not my friends. They are trying to steal me from my mother. That is why she told me not to come. I will pretend to go with them and be good. But I will watch for signs. I will always stay on guard. I will never believe them. When I am able I will return to New York and be with my mother. I need to be with my mother, just the two of us. If we don't take care of each other, who will take care of us? If I don't stay with her, who will stop the computers; who will write letters to the President; who will wash the blood from her scalp? Who will tape the windows when they are broken; who will lie in the bath? Who will sit in the closet, rocking? My fingers in my ears. My fingers in my ears and my eyes. My fingers on my lips.

The Arrival IV

Lisa steps off the bus in L.A. Lili has stayed in New York. Lili is in the bath in the night. Lisa sees the two short people and goes toward them. Lili is in New York with her mother. Lisa dresses for a party in a wool suit her mother made for Lili. At the party Lisa meets Sue. Lili is walking in the snow in New York in a peacoat and a hat. She hears her mother yelling in the apartment in Brooklyn. Lili walks on the streets and pulls at her hair.

Lisa says, "I would like to be a homecoming princess. Or a cheerleader." Lili pulls her scarf around her neck and sings a song as she walks the streets of Brooklyn. It is a song about a boy and a bird. The boy has captured the bird, and the bird begs the boy to let her go because she has babies to feed. *Rachmunis off a mamma.* Have pity on a mother.

Lisa sings, *Loz mich flien*. Let me fly.

Alice Lindsay Price, *Dancing Whooping Cranes*, photograph

Field Guide at Noon

This glare on the fallen sweetgum
trunk. The eye of it, the pupil full.
As though to hoard the light and let it
burn. And then the leaves: star-shaped,
with pointed lobes, and swaying.
This slow, old dance amid the ancient
smells of loam and rot. To believe
like that: to fall to earth then to twitch
again as though alive. The slow hours
of the birds and their desultory songs:
Here is our soft sleep at noon, our drowsy dreams.
Not as though everything has stopped
but close: the way the heart pauses
between beats, lingers. And the wind,
which can barely lift itself from the dirt,
grows snared in the field's tall grass
so can't escape. And what of the heat?
It gathers everywhere like a rebuke:
some sweet-lipped god singeing us
with avenging weight. Surely this is
not what we deserve. And yet we do:
to squint at the canker sore that is
our sun. To stand by this fallen
tree that wants to think it is alive.

Grandchildren of Other Summers

Pipevine, spicebush—
swallowtails fill the four abelias
by my father's road.

One-hundred butterflies,
grandchildren of other summers,
move as if the night sky

were wound tight:
orange globes in triple-digit heat,
the blue just off the moon's edge,

the black of deep space
where nothing returns
to the eye.

One hundred, my son
and father declare,
standing in the road

together, seventy
years apart. I lost
count at thirty-five.

Circulating Like Ghosts in Yellow Light

with apologies to Wallace Stevens

Because there is nothing else,
this is what they anticipate all week
while the disillusionment of ten o'clock
comes sooner and sooner. They slip
into their party clothes and the yellow
light, like fish relieved to be released,
into the pleasures of merely circulating
as if life were motion. The bright
chatter and effusive embraces,
the banal sojourn through the week's gossip,
the wax-work poses —
even the self-appointed outsider
posing simply as Man with Bottle —
all belie a fundamental lack of repose.
The outsider yawns, tips his bottle,
amused to consider himself a scholar
of the anatomy of monotony
as represented by ghosts in a cocoon
of yellow light and perfume.

And truly it is a world without
peculiarity, inhabited by shades who,
on the verge of discovering prologues
to what is possible, retreated
into the safety of supportable half-truths.
Yet the possible continues to stir
just behind the eyes, just under the skin
as they reach toward each other
not knowing what they crave.
Permission? Confirmation?
Not even the outsider wants to go
alone in pursuit of heaven
considered as a tomb or some
esthétique du mal enticingly
warbled by a man with a blue guitar.

On the road home or on the way
to the bus, if it is a clear day
and no memories, they are convinced —
it seems so evident — that the clear sense
of things is exactly what it seems,
like a sea surface full of clouds,
no conundrums, requiring no journey
to the hermitage at the center.
Soothed by the gentle rocking
of the elevator, the buzz of fluorescent
lights, they are like children asleep
in their own lives, and no problems arise
that can't be subdued.

Until, with the fading of the sun,
the old unease waxes, an intimation
that they are men and women that are
falling, each one by himself, by herself,
falling down or up or sideways, into
the terror of mere being,
which propels them toward the yellow
cocktail hour and the men made of words
swimming around each other
to the sad strains of a gay waltz until,
gripped by the desolation of 2 a.m.,
they leak out into the blank night
waving adieu, adieu, adieu.

Drought Conditions

Looking back in the mirror, I saw myself
in the crowd again, among strangers,
trying hard to compose myself
standing in the grass
however dead, this arid September —
clearing my throat for no reason.

I stared back without concern
or interest. One of us counted days,
the other regrets; one laughed, while
the other regarded the cars on the overpass
and began a second count.

We've lived in this desert waiting
for rain so long that the mirages have begun,
along with the cracking of the yellow road paint,
endless lane closures and backups.
The local team will soon begin to drop
easy pop flies. The visions,
these false reflections, offer us not truth,
for they lie as profoundly as the local newspaper,
but a meaning we never expected.

And, looking back, I see finally how shimmery
I have been all this time; how final
and endless it has all been, as far back
as we can go. I held my hand up
in the traffic and again spotted
my double glinting back toward me.

I was surprised how easily I could accept
this shining from everywhere. The city a lake.
My time a dream; my love boundless.

Springdom

April again, sudden dark green
brooding through the season,
anticipating force,

thrumming along the mud lines,
the pulse of a spirit watching us,
coiled and patient,

blood-gorged crocuses and daffodils
witness the robin's swift strokes and
decapitations, the living limbs still wriggling.

The grass blades whisper mutinously,
each one dangerous, reckless, peering out
amidst the chatter of the thrips
and mites.

Every year this same baring
of teeth, this same hunger, under an impatient sky
ready to cry down the riverbeds,
prepare them for the final desolation of July.

Air Conditioning on with the Windows Open

Sometimes in late August this is the only
way to deal with the still strong
sun as it treads its way through
such a pleasant day. Besides,

the curtains and their red berry trim
do a good job of maintaining the cool
while the screen allows the lilting hum
of the day-crickets to serenade me

sitting at the dining room table,
thinking about junctures and seams
joining two entities, and how the afternoon
light this time of year yields a bit more

shadow in the corners of the room
and before you know it, the new season
has arrived, like a car pulling into
your driveway, a wine-dark sedan,

opaque windows, which, after resting uncomfortably
for a few minutes, turns its lights
on in the waning light.

Father and Son

Though a father of two,
the child that needs the most instruction
is the self: that crying, whimpering
dark boy who walks crowds
suspecting everyone, and desiring the attention
of all.

His father was an itinerant preacher,
the kind you read about speaking
by roadsides or near fairs.
I used to listen to him and
wonder who he was, though I
looked through his eyes
at the homely crowds gathered
beneath the locusts, and beyond
at the child alone by
the maples and how he holds his
hands together, sometimes holds mine.

And how I bequeathed to him this
lonely restlessness, that urge to be
just a tuft of grass,
parsimonious and eternal.

Big Georgia and the Sewer

The story has it that when Big Georgia
wasn't yet Big Georgia, but an infant girl
with black curly hair and a cherub's face,
she accidentally crawled into a sewer,
like a pink tongue sliding into a mouth.
She landed in a watery mess of rain
mixed with half-composted pine leaves.
The darkness was nearly complete,
and my sister was unable to reach the top,
to pull herself up, if she even had the power.
It was minutes before my mother noticed
and heard the soft but anguished cries
coming from beneath the street below her.
My mother, already by that time stout
and owning arms stubbier than old pencils,
could not reach down and lift her out.
My sister could see my mother's hand
but couldn't get high enough to touch it.
Stories vary how long she was imprisoned,
some claiming a few minutes and others
most of a full afternoon, but all admit
a rail thin cousin came along eventually,
and with people holding his legs he went in,
grabbed my sister and hauled her to freedom.
Years passed and the story became legendary
to everyone but my sister, who could still
remember being down there with the muck,
calling for help, crying in the dark slimy air,
no light except the thin crack above her
she could not reach no matter how hard
she stretched, she struggled, so she prayed
to grow larger, ever larger, until at last
she could reach the light that God sent in.
She remembered all this in painful detail,
and from that day on, it was said quietly,
she cleaned her plate like a full grown man,
and became bigger and bigger, until Georgia

became Big Georgia, big as the whole state,
big enough she needed nobody's help,
big enough to swallow the entire world
before the world tried to swallow her again.

John Milisenda, *My Mother*, photograph

A Foodish Tale

I imagine myself listening to my nightly struggle
          with onions
as if my mother instead of me stood here
by the counter unwinding the papery skin,
          a sound that
heard at a different time of day
could be so much else instead
a rolling tire
a leaping fish
the voice of someone who shouts too much.
I'll never know how my mother regarded
          onions,
if she relished, as I do, the particular way
they want subduing.
The lack of plot
between the initial grasp from the bin
and the slow revelation,
ends at last
with outright chopping.
No victory, just a small skirmish affirming
sinew of hand and heft in the palm,
friction and squeeze, thub on the board and
oops! protagonist left holding the
first shedding, while the vegetable rolls, just
rolls.
I imagine the onion universe —
about which my present knowledge
does not fill the rind
of half a lemon —
could one day fully emerge
inside the tiny gap
from where I reach
to where I chop,
that place where I always almost lose.

KAROL M. WASYLYSHYN

The Solidity of Fog

He would step into it early
as it tumbled low over the land
but high enough to envelop him
morning scapular
that he could embrace
press onto himself
kiss as a totem
certainty in the quiet,
clarity in the calm
as he worked the right problem
alone in this sudden place
mysterious in its habits
and the fog,
the fog was the only
thing
he
could
trust
completely.

biri

böyle birisi
yüzünün taşlı yollarından, omzundaki yokuştan
denize varıyor nedense
sahilde ıslak kumlara bırakılmış
mavi bir bisiklet buluyor
biri
hem dul, hem bakir
yoksul bir semtin boynundaki atkı

böyle birisi
değişmedi hiç, senin için akşamlara
kurutulmuş çiçeklere, cigara kâğıtlarına
kuşlar çiziktiriyor, kanatsız kuşlar
aynalardan, asılı çamaşırlara vuran ışıktan
çıkmaz sokaklara çıkıyor
biri
hem akıllı, hem deli
bıçak yarası bir sokağın geniş alnındaki

böyle birisi
bir kelebekten ödünç sesiyle
sakalları, kırık kalemleri, ne çok idam
elini soktuğu yastığın altı üşümüş uyurken
korku üşümüş, kış üşümüş, uzakta
ölüp gidiyor herkes yaşarken
biri
hem pul, hem zarf
odasının neminden duvardaki yarımada

böyle birisi
hiç alışık değil gündüzlere, gönül işi
nicedir yaşamasız gecelerde yaşıyor
oyalı mendil, kırgın yazma
bir hastanın iç çekişi sanki
kendinin olmayan bir bulut taşıyor

someone

thus someone
from the stony roads of her face, from the steep way that is on her shoulder
somehow arrives at the sea
finds a blue bicycle
left on the wet sands on the shore
someone
both widow and virgin
the scarf around the neck of a poor neighborhood

thus someone
never changed, and for you, on evenings,
on dried flowers, on cigarette papers
scribbles birds, wingless birds
from the mirrors, from the light that strikes the laundry on the line
goes out to the deadend streets
someone
both reasonable and insane
the knife wound on the broad forehead of the street

thus someone
from a butterfly with a borrowed voice
his beards, his broken pens, so many death sentences
the underside of the pillow where he put his hand, that caught a chill
          while sleeping
the fear caught a chill, the winter caught a chill, far off
goes off and dies while everyone lives on
someone
both stamp and envelope
the peninsula on the wall from the dampness of his room

thus someone
never used to the daytimes, heart work
for how long living in living-free nights
embroidered cushion, angry writing
as if a sick person's sigh
[someone] carries a cloud that is not his own

biri: keman çiziği, kuş teleği, yosunlu dal
biri: çamaşır günleri, bayramlar, bahar gelmiş
biri: ay dökülüyor, hikâye çocukları, kanlı balerin
kurşun askerler ölüyor meydan savaşlarında

hem sen, hem ben . . .
çekilip gidiyor bir tanrı kendi göğünden

one: scratch of fiddle, quill of bird, and mossy branch
one: laundry days, and holidays, and spring has come
one: moon spilling out, and storybook children, and bloody ballerina
lead soldiers dying in heat of battle

and you, and i . . .
a god sneaking away from his own heaven

2005 winter, Kozyatagi — Istanbul

Translated from the Turkish by Donny Smith

Anne Thompson, photograph

acılardan bir abla

gökyüzü ablam olur bulutlu
saçlarını papatyalarla süsleyen
suskun mektuplar alan
hırkalar ören çay demleyen

bir korkuluktur çocukluğum
durur aşkların yanmış bahçesinde
içinde hep korkuların durduğu

elimden tutup
sinemalara gider ablam pazarları
kimi askerlerle bakışlarının çarpıştığı

buzlu camdan kış sabahları
dışarıda yalnız evine dönen
meyhane adamları
bulamam evimin yolunu
pencerede ablam olur

beraber büyümek sonudur
zamanı birlikte geçen çocukların
babamdan gizli sigara içip
avucunda söndüren gül rengi

acılardan bir ablam olur

sister of pain

sky is my sister, cloudy,
who has daisies in her hair,
who receives silent letters
knits sweaters, steeps tea

her childhood is a scarecrow
stays at the burnt garden of the lost loves
fear stays in all the time

my sister, she holds my hand
and goes to cinemas on sunday
where her eyes cross with the soldiers'

on winter mornings, as the frosted glass
drunken men,
coming back home alone
i can't find my way home
and always she is at the window

growing up together is the end
of the children who spend time together
smoking secretly from my father
and putting it out in her palm, the color of a rose

i have a sister, who is of pain

2001 autumn, Tarabya—Istanbul

Translated from the Turkish by Arda Gökçer

93

Indulgences

There's no breeze in this heat, one leaf
in the bush shaking slowly and when my hunger
enters the sky that holds me, it knows no bounds,
flashes forth to encompass every shred of consciousness
I can color Georgia O'Keeffe's numinous

blue. And I remember my favorite saints, Theresa and Joan,
how they offered their suffering up as the nuns
instructed us. But I offer nothing to no one,
strolling by the Ora Sorenson gallery of downtown Delray.
How odd that Ora should hang her huge flowers

in the window just when I'm thinking of Georgia's skulls
in the desert, and how bones are said to contain the soul
of the animal, which is why saints have reliquaries and one
must pay Rome for a toenail, or an "Indulgence" for sin.
I wonder why the old clergy called them "Indulgences"

when they were meant to erase negative stains, meant
as a release from evil? I imagine pastel emanations
rising from shrines, imagine them skating over my skin
like energy orbs, ionizations sanctifying dead horse heads
which hang in Georgia's canvases like the tuba

in Magritte's sky. Georgia made more of the natural objects
in the landscape than I can find in Florida's Caribbean
boutiques. And Magritte certainly knew how two disparate items
juxtaposed become something surreal. Maybe I'm just
tincturing the avenue with my sky-like blues, inherited

genetically from my long-gone father. I'd rather think of him
than my mother whose dementia hangs over her wheelchair

like a stain in her bluish halo, though she won't qualify
for canonization. Now I picture the mantle of "caretaking"
people project over me when it's really *tristesse*

that a life comes to this—not quite cerulean solid
like the pillowy cloud O'Keeffe placed behind the horse's
head, which itself is combed with pinks and browns and yellows,
pale in the long teeth, pleats like liquefying caves,
the shape of mandorlas for birth. And everything

in the estate of my mind's manor is an entrance into blue,
even the punctured holes in the bird's eye view of the skull
as if someone nailed it to the horizon and if I were holier
I just might drop through my mother's strange stigmata
and come out cleansed. One New Year's eve years ago

the two of us killed a bottle of Amaretto and I badgered her
to reveal the truth behind my father's early death. She was still
competent at the time of our argument, but she'd lived the lie
so long she believed it, and I was in therapy, once again
enraged at a man, so I was ruthless. Now that I'm older,

I'm remorseful seeing the atrophy of her sad,
thin body, wishing she'd sprout wings and fly away.
On my bureau there's a photo of us that Christmas under the tree.
We're smiling, tinseled together on my flowered sofa.
Her face is soft and round and feminine, deep

as an O'Keeffe lily, cheekbones still visible like in her youthful
days as a forties airline hostess. My smile is sky-high
and nailed across my face. Our skulls so close together,
how can I *not* see my own fate, how can I *not* look away?
Wrapped in Florida's firmament, no matter how gem-like

its azure, I see O'Keeffe's string-like strokes, the cartilage
of that horse, scaffolding in the sky and my mother's skeletal
shadow. Her husband by his own hand done in, and me
with my bad taste in men, ready to face the desert
of a blank canvas, begin again my next life.

Reading Mark Strand

It's as if he knows how close he's always been to *Spirit*.
As if your hand might pass through the numen of his voice
and a little shadow shiver on the auditorium wall.
If you asked I bet he'd glance away with a half-smile and husky
whisper . . . *Everything ages . . . We grow old . . . Everyone disappears . . .*
and this with a hissing sigh: . . . *Love fades . . . .* But his eyes
would twinkle like wild dice and you'd know underneath
that haunting lives a romantic, why else would he strike us
so droll, and sad and cynical?   One could do worse
than scribble ethereal desires while years slip by

as pages lifted by wind. Maybe he sees something
you can't imagine, what exists beyond ascension —
and always his quavery moans purr like a couple of mongrels,
wounded but playful. *Oh Strand! Oh handsome Strand!*
Your towering gaze hinted at tricks and held out mystery,
a dirigible made out of words, out of reach, a lifeline
we could *almost* grasp as we read the poems built of vowels,
the poems slightly mocking themselves, poems so damn pleased
to be poems, poems bemused at the range of their own pain,
poems consumed with their own toiling well into twilight,

elusive, mewing poems whose feet never touched
ground. And again we're still in the pin-drop quiet, ten deep
in the standing-room-only of his vapory breath. We're almost
splay-legged in rapture while there at the microphone,
he's merely mouthing syllables of light and air and glass,
in the perfectly stitched font of *The New Yorker* in its heyday.
We could sail down the rictus of his cryptic grin, its crescent aisle,
while we cling to his piper's cape and flow from the building
up a Bread Loaf embankment where wind blows color
out of the gloaming and his smoky poems dissolve,

deliquescent as rain beclouding the synchronous rise
of birds, and Strand, with the bittersweet smile, glad
to have touched our lives, never giving a hoot
about who mimicked him . . . he just keeps moving, *holy*

over the fields, an Aquarian Orpheus, one with his head
intact, toes dangling over the edges of our good green planet
into the mythic skies of poetry history, taking his place beside
Homer, Virgil . . . Demosthenes' stones rolling under his tongue,
back to the bicameral tribe, the blue mother cave where
he learned from the silence the most tender language of the born.

Leslie Ringold, photograph

De Profundis

Es ist ein Stoppelfeld, in das ein schwarzer Regen fällt.
Es ist ein brauner Baum, der einsam dasteht.
Es ist ein Zischelwind, der leere Hütten umkreist—
Wie traurig dieser Abend.

Am Weiler vorbei
Sammelt die sanfte Waise noch spärliche Ähren ein.
Ihre Augen weiden rund und goldig in der Dämmerung
Und ihr Schoß harrt des himmlischen Bräutigams.

Bei der Heimkehr
Fanden die Hirten den süßen Leib
Verwest im Dornenbusch.

Ein Schatten bin ich ferne finsteren Dörfern.
Gottes Schweigen
Trank ich aus dem Brunnen des Hains.

Auf meine Stirne tritt kaltes Metall.
Spinnen suchen mein Herz.
Es ist ein Licht, das in meinem Mund erlöscht.

Nachts fand ich mich auf einer Heide,
Starrend von Unrat und Staub der Sterne.
Im Haselgebüsch
Klangen wieder kristallne Engel.

De Profundis

It is a reaped field, in which a black rain falls.
It is a brown tree, which stands alone.
It is a hissing wind, which rounds empty shacks —
How sad this evening.

Past hamlets the meek orphan
Still collects abandoned corn.
Her eyes graze, round and lovely in the twilight;
Her lap awaits the heavenly groom.

On the return home
The shepherds found the sweet body
Decayed in the thorny brush.

I am a shadow far from dark villages.
I drank God's silence
From the grove's well.

Cold metal steps on my brow.
Spiders seek my heart.
A light goes out in my mouth.

By night I found myself on a heath,
Rigid from the star's debris, dust.
In the hazel bush
Crystal angels rang out again.

*Translated from the German
by William Wright and Martin Sheehan*

Rain Dance

We watched the clouds suck moisture
from the atmosphere like an animal
at a water trough and hurried the children
home to park their bikes. The rain began,
a steady shower, and then it sliced across the field
in sheets. Our children danced and shrieked
as the sky's giant sprinkler erupted in a wild riot.
Soon the yard was swallowed in the sound of water
rushing over giddy laughter, pounding
the tin roof awning, gushing down the gutters.
Flowers sighed in the drenching, every muddy stone
echoed the cleansing prattle on their granite.
From underneath the overhang, we witnessed
their marvelous bodies dripping,
ours goose-bumped, dry, fearful
for their wet feet, electric souls. What changed
that made us stay behind the door,
what kept us from going out into the storm
with head tipped back, mouth open, our spirits
reckless with praise and the need to be filled?

Interference

What right do you have to poeticize
the setting sun, drooping roses,
withered ferns, the urgent marching
of the rising and dying natural world?
Isn't it enough for mourning
doves to raise their young in shifts,
the father slipping in through dew
to relieve the hungry mother?
But every scattered acorn,
every broken limb demands
a stanza, some anthropomorphic
significance. Were these objects made
for your scrutiny—after all, why else
do pin oaks cling to leaves
except to demonstrate the way
you hold on to what has passed,
why else do tulips bloom in May
except to celebrate the end
of this season's darkness with a playful
kiss, betrayal sending death hurling
into spring. Fated poet, pause with pen
suspended, permit the wind its awe,
allow the branches their trembling,
consent the earth its holy inhumanity.

Whenever You Arrive

for C

> . . .or as when a bird hath flown through the air, there
> is no token of her way to be found, but the light air
> being beaten with the stroke of her wings, and parted
> with the violent noise and motion of them, is passed
> through, and therein no sign where she went is to be
> found. . .
>
> — *Wisdom of Solomon 5.11*

Whenever you arrive, there is the sound of a storm
beginning in the leaves through a window
I've forgotten is open; I creep to its ledge and watch
the sky steeping over dark clusters of roofs,
the single lights appearing across the river,
and hear faint serpentine melodies shedding their brittle
words, and know I have nothing valuable as these
omens that signal you—all I have
prepared to greet you is this image of you
held delicately, a dry leaf.

Whenever you arrive, across the drifts of tickets,
the gutted envelopes, the sawdust utterances
falling on each spilled face, you spread solstice
over my body, and whisper like a desert shell
remembering the sea. I could not keep from lifting
you once, in the shallows of the sea; we were rocked
as one body by the guileless waves, we were cradled
beyond harm, otherworldly. The thought of it comes
to me now as from a time before my first dream,
whenever your arms circle my earthbound body.

Whenever you arrive, with your footfall
on the stairs like cracking ice, with branches
breaking in your voice, with a past
that serenades you into sadnesses
obscure to me as the source

of the Tiber's mystery, I long to follow
but soon am lost among the tomes of names,
with nothing for my hands
to do but brush a little dust
from the page that's mine.

Whenever you arrive to depart again, to scatter my oaths
among the starless side-lots, to move like a singular ruin
against the sky, then I am done waiting, I am resigned
to the world of brackish attachments, where elsewheres
accumulate like moths around the dimming minds,
where I am nothing but a sagging awning
that suddenly dumps a month of rain, nothing
but the shadow of a curl of smoke climbing a wall—
where everything knows your name is the echo
of a key dropped into the river.

I stood at the bridge's center, having arrived
where I recognized myself beyond reflection
above the flowing silence. Still, I could not
make myself unaware of the maps I traced
on your skin, which may never lead you back.
Whenever you arrive, how will I know
it is you and it is me? Will there be a new
secret we exchange from a place more remote,
more sacred, than memory? Will you be there
when I lay my ear upon the shadow
of your left breast, and hear the ebb and ebb
that draws you slowly down and away from me?
Will there be anything left of me when my voice
follows you again from the room, when all I can do
is reach into the air that closes after you?

Available Life

Look, I've come here with holes
in my pants and my hair strawed by the sun.
I've come through mountains
as dark as a hurricane dusk, through jungle
where vines twine round trees
and insects purr louder than the sea.
I broke through stands of wind-stunted palms,
I wandered down roads of blown dust,
saw white houses with blue roofs,
saw rosebushes, gold sand, and the sea.
I've taken a bungalow here on the shore.
At night I drink warm rum under the wickered cabana,
wander the streets, sit in the ruined lobbies
of empty hotels, where the water, yes I drink the water,
tastes like mold. When I return to my room
it smells of sea-almonds, fresh-cut cherries,
and I feel like the last bee, surrounded by sweetness,
settling to a slow freeze in the sugared comb.
Each night, on the porch, she hangs in the hammock —
quiet, pendant, desirous as a phantom.
She waits, she waits, and I hear her turn
in her sleep like the sea — the sea
that might grant some grace as sure as escape:
a dark harbor beyond shoals of green coral,
wild coffee, bales of black limes,
dew dripping from strange flowers
that feel like flesh.

Adrift

Two nights and a day
we rocked towards shore:
the bow dipped under black waves,
scabs of salt settled on the sail.

Soon we were mumbling:
Zephyrus, Scirocco —
mariners name the winds
so as not to feel lost.

We dreamt of flowers and coconut milk
and on the third night we woke
with bodies bright as burning phosphorus.
We mapped our own constellations into the sea.
Circe, Calypso: islands breached
                         beyond our keel
but the land craved what we could not bear to give.

Like the legends of the Indians tranced into snakes,
we swam when we felt our bodies lost
their limits. Feet into flippers —
eel grass tangled about our heels.
Open water gave way to gray shoals.

Then we landed on shores we did not know
as our own: cry of birds with bright beaks,

rustle and hush of women weaving
through the night.

Obituary for an Asshole

The summer I turned fifteen, my mother's live-in boyfriend invited us to the Toad Suck Fair in Conway, Arkansas. He drove my mother's battered Volvo through nine states, parking at various crossroads only briefly to pee. We ate in the car, slept squished in the back and never stopped to bathe. At night, my brothers and I would fantasize all the different ways we could kill him if we ever got back home. Bruce (who was in high school) came up with the idea of having Earl drawn and quartered—using the dairy herd of Old Man Sweeney who lived a mile from our place.

"We could wait until Earl was asleep and hit him over the head," Bruce whispered. "Then you'd gut him and . . . ."

"I'm not gutting him," I said. "I'm not touching him."

"Me, neither," Danny whispered. Being eleven, Danny was afraid of everything, Earl especially.

"Okay," Bruce continued, "I'll gut him."

"And I'll get the cows," I said. "I can do that."

"Me, too," Danny agreed. "We won't hurt the cows," he continued. "I like cows."

We spent the whole trip perfecting our plan. We didn't have to worry about Earl overhearing us because *he* spent the whole time talking non-stop to our divorcee mother. That's because Earl was on uppers and was fleeing to Arkansas until things calmed down in Humptulips, which was a fifty-cent-sized hamlet nestled in the most rural of foothills in Washington State's Olympic Mountains.

When we finally got to Arkansas and met Earl's mother and father we could see why he was so awful.

"God Almighty, you're sure a fatty," Gramma Lambini said to my mother, before turning to my brothers and me. She looked us up and down and spit tobacco juice over the porch rail. Apparently, we weren't worth an insult, which was, in some bizarre and twisted way, even worse than being called a fatty.

Mother immediately telephoned our father. I never knew what she told him, but he sent enough money via Western Union to buy three bus tickets back to Seattle. Only Danny grieved the loss of attending the Toad Suck Fair. He wanted cotton candy, corn dogs, deep-fried Snickers bars and a white t-shirt with "Welcome to the Ozarks" on the front and a green, goggle-eyed, bouncing frog on the back.

"We could ride the Zipper and watch the pig races," Danny whined. He was good at whining and he put his heart into it but Gramma Lambini told him to shut the fuck up and he did, shocked that an old lady would actually use the F Word.

"It isn't fair that Mom gets to stay," Danny whined as we wrestled our sleeping bags from the back of the station wagon and rolled them tightly for our trip to the bus depot in Conway.

"Don't be a dork," my older brother muttered and for the first time in weeks, I agreed with him.

"Yeah," I said, "don't be a dork."

"Shut the fuck up," Gramma Lambini shouted from inside the house. So we did.

Obituary — Draft One

I learned about Earl's death from my mother. Her email was to the point. "He always wanted to go home to Arkansas. I know you'll do the right thing, Sharon."

Notice that, at twenty-seven, I was the right-thing girl while she was in France with her new daughter-in-law and newer grandbaby. I placed an international call to my brother, Bruce, who was learning to be a sous-chef at Le Cordon Bleu. "Are you and Mother coming to the funeral?"

"Don't be an idiot."

"So, I'm supposed to handle this on my own?"

"Danny can help."

"Shit," I said. "You are going to owe me big time."

"Add it to your Big Brother's Big Time List." There was a pause. "Seriously, send me the bills. All of them."

"Guilt can be expensive," I said. "Any ideas for the obituary?"

"Earl's an Asshole. Isn't that enough?"

Obituary — Draft Two

I spent three hours driving from Seattle to the home of my childhood—a place without electricity. After Danny and I unpacked and fed Earl's bluetick hound, named Sam, I sat at Mother's battered kitchen table, fingers twitching with anticipation. The doublewide trailer was steamy with the heat from a woodstove. There was a kerosene-powered refrigerator with only one photo on the fridge door. It showed a towhead with brown eyes and a smile that could break your heart. It had hung there the whole time we'd all lived with Earl and he'd never explained. To be fair, we'd never asked but we weren't a family that used conversation to communicate.

I picked up a pencil and after drawing a tombstone and a hangman's tree, I warmed up with my own obituary, using a sheet of paper torn from my daily planner.

Sharon died surrounded by her children, grandchildren, and one tiny namesake great-granddaughter. She was predeceased by her mother and older brother, Bruce. Her younger brother, Danny, gave the eulogy.

Danny leaned over me to read. "Where's Ralph?"

Apparently I had forgotten my husband but perhaps he had gone ahead of me because of the male-female thing. Still it gave me a chill. "This is practice," I said. "It's to get me in the mood."

"You don't want to be in the mood for Ralph?"

There were so many responses to make that I was overwhelmed with opportunity and sat a moment, trying to sort things out. I tore three more pages from the back of my day planner. It wasn't until I was deep into Earl's obituary that I realized the first three letters in funeral spelled "fun" and I tried to keep that in mind as the paper soaked up the ink.

Earl was an asshole, who abused our mother, assaulted her children, and lied at every opportunity. No doubt the town of Humptulips will have a memorial potluck at the Grange Hall where the men will remember what a good poker player Earl was and the women will bring elk meat and noodle casseroles. The men will shoot off some guns and everybody will drink themselves blind in his honor.

The words flowed easily, as if I'd thought about them my whole life, which, truth be told, I pretty much had. I put on my coat and took the obituary down to the little white church to be copied. Ole Knutson, the choir director, proofread it and said, "There's no need to make fun of us, Sharon. Just because you went off to college doesn't mean the rest of us are damn fools."

I wadded up the smudged piece of paper and dropped it in the wastebasket by the door. Writing is about revision. I'd try again tonight, when I wasn't up to my armpits in sorting and packing Earl's crap.

"I'll do better."

"See you do."

"He was an asshole," I said. "That part is true."

"Yes, but he was our asshole and, once upon a time, your mother loved him."

Obituary — Draft Three

Danny was growing a mustache. He looked fearless but looks were deceiving and he thought he was going to die whenever he stepped into an airplane. "I hate flying."

"Then stay home."

"You're mean."

"No, I'm not. When we're done here, I'm taking Earl, a complete piece of crap, to be buried with his kin. Some people would call me a saint."

"You don't want Mom to cry."

Hard to argue with that. I tore more blank sheets from my journal. "You lived with Earl longer than I did, help me out."

Danny scuffed his feet and flexed his muscles. He almost looked his age, twenty-four years and four months. His anti-psychotic medication was working and he almost sounded sane, too. "Well, he liked to hunt and fish."

Okay, maybe the key to writing an obituary was to not do it yourself. Maybe a person had to have a little help. At the top of the sheet of paper I wrote, <u>Earl was an outdoorsman.</u>

"What else?"

"He liked fishing."

"Anything else?"

"And he had a girlfriend."

"No, he didn't."

"Everybody knew it, Sharon. Even Mom."

"That was just a rumor."

"They had a little girl. Sometimes Mom would baby-sit when Olivia was working nights."

I wadded up the paper from my journal and threw it into the flames of the kitchen stove. I was stuck writing an obituary for a man who was slime. Not to mention the idiocy of my mother for putting up with it all those years.

I went outside to stand on the porch. The snow had turned blue under a sky the color of apricots. I stood there until stars pricked through a darkening sky. Soon the eyes of predators and of prey would wait for the truth only night could bring. If I had to choose, I would be a predator, sharp of fang and fierce of claw, but my mother's face was always there as a reminder that sometimes things didn't turn out the way you wanted. Sometimes you started out as predator and ended up as prey.

The whine of a logging truck, making a last run to the mill, cut through the twilight like a chainsaw against second growth. The air on the porch was cold enough to make my eyes sting and my nose run. An owl drifted silently past the henhouse, hoping for poultry's innate stupidity to provide the feast. Hoping for a bird to act like a human.

The cold helped for some reason; the involuntary shivering froze out the hate, turning it into ice crystals that shattered and fell like fine snow around my feet. Danny came out and wrapped me in a blanket. "You have to come in now," he said.

"No, I don't."

"I made toasted cheese sandwiches and tomato soup."

"I'm not hungry."

"I'll tell Ralph you aren't eating."

Ralph was my husband, the man I could not include in any obituary, no matter how imaginary. He was a good man, sweet, who was going to come with me this weekend but had orals for his doctorate. "Fuck orals," he'd said. "You're more important than them."

"We're having a child," I'd replied. "Quit thinking like a husband and start thinking like a father who has to get a job."

Obituary — Draft Four

Danny talked to Ralph over the battery-powered telephone because cell towers still hadn't made it this far into the foothills. It was like talking to someone on the moon, or in the Alaska bush, because of the relay delay. I was at the table, still wrapped in the blanket, a mug of soup in my hand. I shook my head and pulled the blanket tighter around me. Danny shifted the receiver from one hand to the other. "She won't come to the phone." He had to wait a slow count to five before Ralph answered—loud enough for us both to hear.

"Why not?"

"This obituary is hard to write."

The static was like electric popcorn on a red-hot skillet, then came Ralph's calm voice. *"Earl Lambini, Born August 12, 1950. Died from a gunshot wound sometime in February, 2010. Found three weeks later. Memorial Service Sunday after church.* That's all she needs."

"You know Sharon," Danny said.

Ralph sighed and hung up.

Obituary — Draft Five

It was morning and I was in the Grange Hall parking lot, loading the remains of Earl's life into the shed that held donations for the Clothing Bank. I wrestled five black garbage bags filled with plain flannel shirts and leaky olive green hip-waders. Danny was back at the doublewide, stuffing empty beer cans into plastic bags. Danny could have Sam, the hound, but I didn't know what to do with the chickens. Thinking about it made me tired.

A green and white Blazer turned off Highway 101. Locals liked to say Sheriff Posey was a good man but a little soft in the heart when it came to kids. "Kids don't got a choice," the Sheriff had once said. That terse sentence, in country shorthand, covered it.

He cracked the window and cigarette smoke rolled out like fog over a forest fire. "I expected to see your mother. She always cleaned up after Earl. How's she doing?"

"Mom's in France, visiting Bruce and her new grandbaby." The Sheriff would remember my older brother, having busted him for pot on more than one occasion.

"And Danny?"

"Danny's living with me and taking his medication. He's fine and dandy. Fit as a fiddle. Happy as a pig in shit." It was funny how the homilies, the country descriptions of behavior, all came back.

Sheriff Posey tamped down a new cigarette, scratched the match alive with his thumbnail and cupped his hands around the flame. He inhaled and let the smoke dribble from his mouth. "How are you, Sharon?"

"I'm fine."

"Looks like you got a bun in the oven." Sheriff Posey was a no-bullshit guy and, once upon a time, I had dated his youngest son. He rolled the window down further. "Need a hand?"

"No, I'm done for now. I heard about Mrs. Posey. I'm sorry. She was a good person."

"That she was."

We stared at each other for a beat. Nobody can outstare a cop so I asked, "What do you want?"

His hair and beard were almost all white. He was probably close to retirement. "You know the story of how Earl died?"

"He committed suicide in one of his hunting blinds."

"The state cops aren't so sure about that."

"Why not?"

"It was a gut shot, Sharon. Suicides don't generally go out with that much pain. Coroner figures it took him twenty-four hours to die."

"I didn't do it."

"Glad to hear it."

"My brothers didn't, either." I stuffed another bag of Earl's clothes into the church's shed.

"Nobody hated him worse," the Sheriff said. "You can see how I had to ask."

"I understand."

"Then I'll be getting back to the office."

On impulse I blurted out, "I'm trying to write Earl's obituary. You wouldn't have any ideas, would you?"

"He was one of a kind," the Sheriff said. "Thank God for that."

After he left, I scribbled the Sheriff's words onto the back of a bank deposit slip, *Earl was one of a kind and thank God for that*, then I headed for the Mercantile to pick up a cheap tablet. No sense wasting any more daily planner pages or deposit slips on rough drafts.

Obituary — Draft Six

It was a country store, with groceries in the front and a restaurant in the back. Sam stocked shelves with an economy of motion that could only be learned from doing the job forty years in a row. Gertie, the cook, scraped the grill in preparation for another day of burgers and homefries.

"What'll it be?" A cigarette dangled from Gertie's mouth, its ashes sprinkling over the hash browns like an exotic kind of pepper.

"Three burgers with onions, one for here and two to go."

"You want cheese fries?"

"You know I do."

I ate my burger and fries at a table surrounded by mismatched chairs. A group of snowmobilers stumbled in, faces red with cold and excitement. They headed for a back booth and Olivia took them a pot of coffee and a handful of menus.

Sam and Gertie owned the Mercantile and Olivia was their daughter, an ex-cheerleader who, fourteen years before, had gotten sidetracked by the high school basketball star. Now she had two kids by two different fathers and a desperate look about the eyes that meant she was sick to death of living with her parents.

The bag of take-out was greasy with flavor and I collected extra napkins. Olivia rang up the bill and followed me out the door. A pair of eagles spiraled in a lazy double helix above the river.

Olivia sucked on her cigarette. "Earl had cancer."

"I didn't know that."

"I loved him even if he was a sonofabitch and I didn't shoot him, no matter what that damn Sheriff Posey says."

"He asked half the people in the county," Sam's voice was muffled from inside the store. "Don't go getting all ruffled up about it."

"Earl told me he didn't want to die in a hospital. I went up and fed the dog and chickens." Olivia shoved an envelope into my shirt pocket. "He gave me this before he did it. He said you'd know what to do. I would have mailed it but I didn't have your address."

I drove a full mile before swerving the Jeep to the shoulder and opening the envelope. The printing inside was labored and every word was a single syllable.

"Take me to Toad Suck Park and put me with my son. Drop my hand-tied flies in with me, too."

I pulled a U-turn and parked in front of the store. Olivia was still on the porch, but she'd moved further down and away from the door.

I climbed awkwardly from the Jeep, caught between anger and confusion. "What son?"

"The only person he ever loved. The one he gut-shot by mistake when they went hunting up in the Ozarks twenty years ago."

It was clear that the fun had drained right out of the word funeral. We stood together, watching the eagles, until Olivia's cigarette was down to the filter. "My life is shit," she whispered. "Every morning I wake up and Sam's stomping around and Gertie's nagging and I feel like I'm drowning."

We stood together for a long time. Sam stuck his head out but ducked it back in when he saw Olivia's look. Living in the back of the store was taking its toll on all of them.

"If you handle the service and write Earl's obituary," I said, "you can have the trailer and everything that's in it. You can have the dog and the chickens, too. All of it is yours. Every damn thing."

"What about taking him down to Arkansas?"

"Danny and I will handle that."

Tears in her eyes, Olivia nodded. If we were men, we would have shaken hands on it or pounded shoulders but we were women not close enough to hug so I handed her two napkins, one with my phone number and the other to blow her nose on. I climbed back into the Jeep and put it into gear. I picked up Danny and headed for Seattle. He wolfed down his burgers and shared his fries while I told him the plan. "Okay," he kept saying. "Okay."

Obituary — Final Draft

Conway, Arkansas, was caught in the crosshairs of Interstate 40 and Interstate 65. The best IHOP in the south nestled like a tick on an old hound that was wrapped around that busy intersection, kicking out a leg and growling now and then but mostly dozing away the hours. I'd rented a Subaru at the airport. I had Earl's ashes under the passenger seat and Danny had the hand-tied flies on his lap in a metal Altoids box.

"We'll have blueberry crêpes when we're done," I said.

"Okay," Danny answered. I was liking this new medication and living with him wasn't so bad, lately, since most of what he said was "Sure" and "Okay" and sometimes "Good idea."

We stood below the dam where the banks were overhung with cottonwoods and raggedy pines. Danny pointed out some mosquitoes skating on a moss-green pool and a catfish barely broke the surface for a morning snack. I dumped the plastic bag of ashes and said "Good-bye" without adding "Good Riddance," which was as close to making peace with Earl as I would ever get. Danny tossed in the hand-tied flies and we watched the current carry them downstream.

The Lambini homestead was at the end of a single-track lane. I've wondered why, long ago, an Italian had homesteaded at the south end of the Ozarks but immigrants have spread all over this broad land, so why not amid piney woods and croaking toads?

Earl's mother had a face like an apple left on the tree all winter, wizened, limp and scabby, but still all of one piece. His father sat sullenly in the porch rocker, with a steady creak-creak to mark his days. Old-timer's Disease was what Gramma Lambini called it.

Her expression didn't change when we told her Earl was dead.

"Did he leave me anything?" she asked.

Danny and I played eyeball ping-pong but neither of us mentioned the trailer in Humptulips. I told her where we scattered Earl's ashes, expecting her to say something soft and sad so I was a little surprised when she said, "He always was a bum."

Probably Earl hadn't been a six-year-old bum or even a twelve-year-old one but bumhood might have caught up with him by the age of thirty. Shooting his own son could fill a man with enough hate that a self-inflicted gut shot might not seem like such a bad idea. The cancer was just an excuse. I handed Earl's mother his obituary and headed for the car.

"You spelt my name wrong," she said. "And who the hell is Olivia?"

I didn't turn around. From birth to death our lives are only half-told and half-understood, too. Beyond Earl's final resting place, IHOP waited with bacon, blueberry crêpes, black chicory coffee, and a friendly face or two.

Earl Lambini was the son of Charlene and Jefferson Lambini, originally of Toad Suck, Arkansas. He was predeceased by his nine year old son, Earlie, Jr. Earl died by his own hand sometime in February of this year. He leaves his fiancée, Olivia, and their daughter, Ashley.

My Mother's Teeth

You had been held without effort and with indifference
for two full days in the soil's untidy grip before

I found them in the small round Tupperware
on the shelf above your sink. Those pale, low
battlements against which your words were born.

I say the body's ferocity to die is as real
as its ferocity to live. I remember the way
the firm seam of your lips refused every

effort we made to feed you tiny portions of food
and crushed tablets folded with honey.
I knew the undertaker had packed your throat

with gauze, caulked your mouth
to a pleasing shape and then wired your jaw
finally closed and I began dreaming

you'd been kidnapped, your mouth stuffed
with whatever was close at hand—scarf, sock,
underwear, duster—because it felt as if the world

were holding you ransom; as if a typed note
would drop through the galvanized sneer
of the letter box; that whatever the price,

I would pay it. We had cleared the paraphernalia
of your dying away: the baby food and morphine
and needles. The bed. The commode. The dressings

and tablets and fortified juices, and the oxygen
with its skeins of tubing. And because I needed
to hold them fast, in the way I held your body

fast, in mind, in the earth, with your feet
to the hills and your head to the bay and its small talk
of salt, I climbed to the lake with your teeth,

in their plastic temple, in my pocket.
You must remember how it is: the higher
you climb, the deeper the world inhabits

its essentials until there is nothing
but wind and brightness, hand in hand, heaving
through the ling and bog cotton; and,

close to the soil, the solid-green mouths
of the sundew, which never truly close, building
their sweetness out of rain and light and the rendered

bodies of insects. And I threw them in: I threw
your teeth into the silken grip of the water,
which treasures everything it is offered—even tannin

and shadow, even the droppings of sheep
like dark round buttons, even bones unbuckled
in the heather. I say the mouth

is the most dangerous kingdom of all. I say paradise
is there behind the gates of the teeth because
it is there that the tongue's nimble wand

names its hungers. And I say life means nothing
if we can't be brought willingly down and consumed
by the terrible needs in another's mouth.

There were warriors once who pried
the teeth from every defeated adversary simply
to ensure that with his mouth plundered

and his words unformed each man would walk
unarmed into the next life. Just think
what such a belief reveals about the purpose of words

in this life. But I say even in this life, sometimes,
there is no language. Only gesture. I threw them out
as far as I could. I say the living can be wounded

like water. With a final, shy sound they slipped through
the skin of the lake. And I kissed them, of course,

before I threw them. Of course. Of course I held them,
gently, and with both hands, and I put them to my lips.

Kathryn Dunlevie, *Home*,
archival pigment print on panel, 8.5" x 8.5"

Navigation

> The spiritual problem is death—only death. The
> technical problem, which is an index to the spiritual
> one, is how to write about it.
>
> —*Edward Hirsch*

Chart and Compass

Month after month, every morning, on a tray
painted with water colors of chives and agrimony
and of lavender, my father brought her orange juice,
a cream serviette and a silver cruet; brought her
a dish of multi-colored tablets, vibrant
and garish as aquarium gravel; brought her the moist,
diminutive rubble of a scrambled egg, and a slice
of toast, buttered and cut into four neat squares
and placed, carefully, the tough keels of the crusts
removed, at the four points of the compass on the rim
of a large white dinner plate. I would think, then,
about the charts of the old explorers, of how the known
world gives way to a numb, white reach
of parchment across which animals, half-feathered,
half-scaled, each covering more than one possibility,
float; across which someone, with a flourish
of exquisite penmanship, once wrote *There Be Dragons
Here.* And how could there not be. I imagine the terror
was never of such blankness itself, but of how
it marked not the ending, but the beginnings
of something. Imagine your little ship reaching
a border such as this, crossing it, and sailing
on; the way a new world acquires its language
out of the widening cut of your wake: the way
love does, or despair. And every morning, month
after month, with the details of the previous day
flushed away, once more, through the nets
of memory, my mother was newly surprised
and delighted because the last time she'd eaten
a scrambled egg in her pyjamas, she said,

was in Hampstead, in school, during the war,
weakened by fever, when the nuns served
her breakfast in bed in a sickroom with windows
looking out over a tongue of lawn that swept
away toward ordered rows of war-effort vegetables
and the dark-churned mouth of the Sisters' duck pond.

Astrolabe

This was the era of siren suits, stepped into
and zippered, before the whole school filtered
down into the cellar of the new gymnasium
to lie shoulder to shoulder, the soles
of their feet against the cellar walls, and wait
out the nightly raids of German bombers;
a breathing fringe of beige reciting
Latin verbs, the room's acoustics gifting
the words with a second body; like seeing double,
my mother said, but through sound. Each word
with its following ghost. She remembers
the night the Sisters' pond took a direct hit
from a bomb discarded by a damaged Heinkel;
and even though I know they were herded
at night into wooden huts by the garden plots,
I needed to hear her say it; I needed to know
she remembered, still, the Aylesburys
and white Campbells spilling out into daylight
and floating all day in the flooded crater
of the pond. By the time she was able to sit
up in bed and eat her scrambled duck egg, that pond
was a pond once more, behaving the way
water behaves under various kinds of light; but, she said,
in her fever the ducks had appeared and disappeared
like the flak of something holy and the pond
had been a bright tack keeping the tongue
of the lawn in place under the wind, a fresh coin
for the boatman. There were the mornings

Direct Observation

I lay next to her just to see what she saw:
rectangle of lawn, and the spine of the hedge
twitching in the wind, its foliage, like youth,
giving the world a false permanence; high up,
the wind-lashed beauty of jet trails
unzipping; in the garden, on the line, the heave
and gloat of pegged washing. The clutter
of finches and sparrows at the feeder, and,
in the northwest corner of the garden,
where the hedges almost met, that galvanized
gate through to rough ground where my father
piled his clippings—the lawn's total wealth—
and the mountain ash with its sporadic
shade and its red spittle of berries. Sometimes
a storm working through its various stages
of undoing. And sometimes I would catch her
pulling back the wide cream sleeves of her silk
pyjamas to stare in disbelief at those places
where her body had run aground, hard,
against its own surface—the bruising chatter
of medicines and illness. And sometimes,

Sounding Line

even though she was tethered by the transparent
hooks of the cannula, there was so much extra
tubing that she could move from room
to room, entering each room. And, watching her,
how could I not think of Theseus, his spool
of thread uncoiling through the bewildering
maze behind him as he kept on wading
forward, into darkness. But once
she had woven herself through the house
until every room was strung on a clear reed
of plastic, my mother would simply turn around
and undo her journey.

121

Marking One's Position

Now, summer is pouring slowly out of its traces,
and I dream that my mother, wrapped up
in some extravagant emerald dress, is withdrawing
herself from the room of every leaf, her long green light
running out over the threshold. I wake in panic, believing
that while I was sleeping even my words
had slipped from the mouth of every poem as the gods

withdrew their tongues. Because hers was the house
that contained the door that was my entrance

into this world. And whatever gods there are lay claim
to pieces of her body and yet they have left me with nothing

but that body. And there was her plunge
into sleep, and the rising up again.
                                    Until there wasn't.

Counting Backwards

How did I get so old,
I wonder,
contemplating
my 67th birthday.
Dyslexia smiles:
I'm 76 in fact.

There are places
where at 60 they start
counting backwards;
in Japan
they start again
from one.

But the numbers
hardly matter.
It's the physics
of acceleration I mind,
the way time speeds up
as if it hasn't guessed

the destination—
where look!
I see my mother
and father bearing a cake,
waiting for me
at the starting line.

Hospice Tape #3

Miracles of technology throttle me
less than they do my father, who wept
to see my mother, two weeks dead,

on the camcorder flip-screen,
the flickering stamp of her gaunt face.
She spoke about God and absence,

looking for one in the other,
learning to love my father
only after she had left.

Someone told me an adult life
does not begin until you see a parent die
and know it's possible.

Needle-draws and hospital gowns,
liquid pixels and high-definition,
always light, this aperture for grief.

I rewound to where I was a child,
paused. My father left for his study,
those quiet offices fathers keep.

Tools

My father owns three ball-peen hammers
I've never seen him use, a crosscut saw
we dulled taking down a half-dead oak.

He has a sickle we passed back
and forth to clear nettles and tall grass
when we plotted our white-washed shed

built to hold more tools, where we keep
the bolt-cutters he used to hack
through the holly bushes, to get under

the porch where our old dog crawled.
The mangled hollies didn't survive winter.
Lined up along the shed wall you can see

the rusted machinery we need even
when we don't: rake, shovel. We clear
a corner for a pruner picked from a yard sale.

Every year the shed seems smaller, closer
to the brim. We keep accumulating,
stacking what we find on what we forget.

The Bull Moose

I

Earliest faint of dawn, lip-slip
silence of river
and like a fish opened
the sky bleeds and feathers
as three moose feed
in the slackwater by the islands,
dark silhouettes
among the bales of mist.

II

Three hours later and the day
is tiled in sun, gleaming heat.
The bull moose has followed a feeder stream uphill
and my father goes to find it.
I too set out,
after a strange moment's peace,
to seek
in those tunnels of green.

III

Arms raked by pines and the stream
lost among skirts of moss
I relent, nothing found
and nothing to find,
held
in a sun-fluted jar of day, shadow-pocked
ark of soul through which
silently the great shapes tumble.

Tonight

In memory of Jiri Orten, 1919-1941

I wanted to make something
beautiful for you, reader,
to arrange words on a page
as if they were pure yellow leaves
plucked from smoky October.
But today a woman told me
a story about a man:
told me how decades ago, in a granite city,
he was dragged by a car,
then left at a hospital where doctors
refused to admit him
because he was Jewish.
I don't know if those doctors, long dead,
are free from nightmares tonight.
Or how long, denied morphine,
it took for the man to die.

I am thinking of what a saint said
about a different crucifixion: that its mystery
was reserved for the future.
Francis knew time was fluid, but like the rest of us,
flinched from pain.
In middle age, before his eyes were cauterized,
he asked the fire to be kind.

Tonight, I believe
those blue flames listened. I believe
if we pray hard enough,
rivers can flow backward.

He was an artist, the woman told me,
and he was young.
Let us kneel, tonight, beside his ruined body.
Let us stay with him.

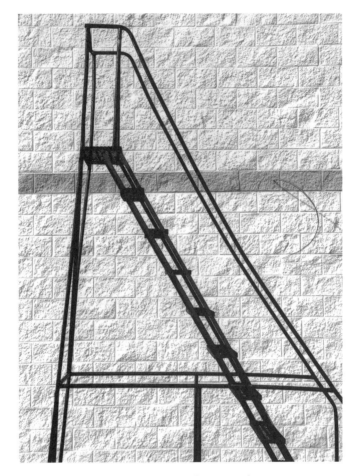

Mark Weiss, photograph

Southwest History Class

I confiscate Antonio's rolls of flavored candy:
Dubble Bubble,
fruit punch,
cola,
Jolly Rancher,
strawberry kiwi.

While he reads the chapter
on Spanish borderlands,
I read the candy labels,
curled from riding all morning
in the pocket
of his *Virgin de Guadalupe* hoodie.

Antonio is what one would call disruptive,
full of belches, f words,
finger tapping, book dropping,
one whose desk
vibrates like a metal sorceress.

When I tell the class that the Spanish
allied with the Ute,
while the Apache remained hostile,
he tells me he is half-Indian,
half-Mexican.
What nation? I ask.
I don't know, he replies
scratching the raven tattooed
on his neck.

The students continue to read
about Spanish colonizers, Coronado,

Cabeza de Vaca, Juan de Ulibarri,
Oñate, though this history book
doesn't mention that he cut off
the left foot of Acoma males
to keep them in the colony.

As I prepare the next lesson,
the French coming up from Louisiana,
the room fills with restless
sounds, muffled whispers, crinkled notes,
pencils scratching, an occasional
spitball, and the intermittent
Scotch Tape dispensing from its roll
with a strangled zip.

Bahala Na: Delano 1965

> Fiction is history . . . or it is nothing. But it is also more
> than that; it stands on firmer ground . . . whereas history is
> based . . on second hand impression.
> —*Joseph Conrad*

At night on Main Street—red lights
string muted rubies in the Tule fog,
histories of Three Card Monte, Acey Deucy, in Mochi's Bar,
shy visits to Lola's place behind the Starlight bowling alley,
cockfights, and knife fights retold in Tagalog and pidgin English,
Escrima dreams, *Bahala na*, whatever happens, happens.
Lucky Lucay, Julian Balidoy, Rudy Sulite, Angel Cabales,
winners of Purple Hearts, Silver Stars and government commendations,
those scouts, point men, and coast watchers,
those slick-haired boys who jitterbugged in pre-war Manila,
who dove for oysters with goggles made from glass bottle bottoms,
in the lagoons of Cebu and Mindanao,
who led G.I.s from Texas and South Philadelphia
through the bamboo jungles.

Now they walk toward vanishing points and perimeters,
pruning shears slung over their shoulders instead of carbines.
The straw boss can't get their names right.
Asparagus knives and Texas shorties
in hands as hard as the soles of your shoes.
They water gardens of winter squash and bitter melon.
Men without women, behind the barracks in the labor camp,
cook *adobu* in outdoor kitchens in Earlimart and Delano,
fieldpack the ladyfingers, *ribeiras* and flaming reds.
It's piecework, Little Rudy, so pick them and pack them fast,
then nail the lugs shut and swamp them
into cold storage, reefer trucks, to go south over Tejon Pass

through Castaic Junction into another valley.
Angel Cabales could hammer the fruit crates shut
faster than the machine that killed John Henry,
the seeds still warm, the flesh of the fruit still trembling.

Now in winter, in the thick Tule fog
they walk the picket lines in army surplus parkas,
outside the entrance to the Di Giorgio Ranch.
Anting Anting tattoos fade on their calves and chests.
Blood tugs from their limbs back to their hearts.
They huddle around fires in fifty-gallon barrels,
remembering their women, they dream
histories of Lapu Lapu, the warrior king,
who killed Magellan in his armor, in the shallows,
with a fire-hardened wooden stick and a bow and arrow.

During the strike, I hung around the edges of their fires,
warmed my hands, darkened
my soft face over the smoking drums,
installing in my silent ear the braveries of others.
Now I try and reconstruct it all, try to get it right,
but I was a boy looking at the world of men
through his thick horn-rimmed glasses.

But they still tell the story in Mochi's bar
of Angel Cabales in the Giumarra cold storage,
fighting his way through five Anglos
and laying them out cold
with a twenty-two-inch bamboo *escrima* stick.
Rudy Sulite, Julian Balidoy, Lucky Lukay,
those slick-haired island boys who carried
their Silver Stars and faded Purple Hearts
in beat-up wicker suitcases from labor camp to labor camp,
are as real, now, as this poem,
who stand on firmer ground than history.

Escrima: Filipino martial art
Anting Anting: Religious/good luck charms
Texas shorties: Short-handled hoes
Bahala Na: As God wills; also used to mean one will meet any challenge; the motto
of one of the units of Filipino soldiers that were part of the U.S. Army during
World War II

Why I Remember

In memory of Bruce Elwin McGrew

> *Stories are like scars holding us to our wounds*
> *until we understand them well enough to heal*
> *whatever it is in us calling the enemy against us.*

1.
I charge these scrawls in a swelter of oils and turpentine
roiling through this studio lent by my old friend Bruce,
sizeable Scot I first met when he crept conspicuously
into the Sonoran auditorium where I was declaring

the storm of my early poems—him in his tartan kilts
and leopard skin, big bass drum and warrior's grin.
And still all these years later I will marvel
at how this wild beauty warrior's nuanced figures

reconfigure the old barnwalls—women of nubile light
mutable as clouds, shapeshifting fishmen,
aureolean chariot, bulls in sexual bloom—
while he's off sketching reflections from Lake Patzcuaro.

2.
Before heading out last night for another's reading,
I propped up your small watercolor of the coast at Moclips
remembering how I first saw that place March 1960
from a metallic blue, oil-spewing '52 Ford ragtop

out to escape my first and last formal philosophy class —
the T.A., pompous, logical, humorless and shrewd,
claimed Socrates was committed to suicide by "rules
as clear and binding as baseball's." I remember because
as the sun went down as it's going down in your painting
a car behind me came up flashing its lights and honking
until I pulled to the side. Two guys came up, got confused,
thought I was somebody else who drove a blue convertible

too fast with wild dark hair, then they asked me
back to see what they had in their car, and I,
because I was stupid, a couple years older, bored,
considerably more sober, I went, wondering what a pair

of Indian kids could want from me and too curious to resist.
When they opened the back door, there was their sister, they said,
and they kept mumbling something I kept not understanding
until one, reaching in, lifted her skirt. She stared up,

eyes out of focus, asking over and over, "Whoozzis? Zisshim?
Who you toll me bout?" The boys, pulling Rainier beers
from their stash in a paper bag, offered me a can,
asked how much I had, asked if I

wanted a date with their sister, and she, reeking,
who couldn't quite sit up, was asking her question
over and over. Speechless, unnerved, I drove off
head whirling into the night, wondering what madness

in lives so young could drive them to this, lives
lived so far from the stupefying urban frenzy I'd
come here to escape, looking for nothing but a beach
to sleep on — top down to full moon and falling stars,

Socrates a renegade still alive and well in my heart,
radio crooning, "All I have to do is dream, dream, dream,"
smells of surf and seaweed anchoring me to earth. So
I looked at your watercolor again — its ingenious beauty,

blue puddled on tan sand, water rising green, sky
a fan of gray and blue cut by streaks of raw salmon—
and I remembered that girl, and I remembered the two boys
scarcely old enough to drive, all dying drunk, raven hair

blueblack in their faces, eyes darker than mine, bargaining
first for their sister and then for what was left
of their beer; and how beautiful that night had become
out under the stars, alone, the same stars those three

were born under, same sea they'd grown up hearing,
and I remember wondering what kind of dreams they
must keep sheathed sharp and deep in their hearts.
I was still wondering last night, driving into the city

to hear a Navajo poet read, just about the age
those boys' sister would be, if she lived—a poet
whose work I knew but wished to hear aloud myself,
30 years later. And I heard as she blessed her daughters

with first-day-of-spring and first-day-of-school songs,
heard her chide a friend for her "bad news" boyfriend,
a Navajo cowboy with raisin eyes and pointed boots.
I heard as she spoke of her own younger brother, dead,

buried, as she said, "in the strength of ageless songs,"
heard as she sang, beginning, *"Ashenee shishili"*
like the rustling of cornstalks just before rain,
ending, "It is as you predicted: we go on."

3.
When she pauses, looking up to whisper
in a voice as politic as silk rubbing silk, "This is
something we all know on Reservations,
but I don't think they tell you. . . ." And she tells:

A young Navajo whose gas-pump jammed in Farmington
paid and started to drive off when through the rear window
he was shot by a clerk demanding 97 cents extra
"for the spill-over," a clerk later fined

for discharging a firearm within city limits
and fired for violating company policy.

"Our lives," she croons,

". . . not even worth a dollar."

4.
In the years since that night, I've thought, sometimes,
of that girl, thin legs spread like a child's
in the backseat, eyes muddled by beer and a future
incomprehensible at the time. And why I remember her

is not for an image lost in twilight but for the times
I've worried about her since then, whenever I see a woman
in that kind of trouble, with that kind of brother at hand.
And because I know such changes in fortune as I wish her

cannot simply be given, must be discovered—by luck, by faith
persevering but on a scale so hard for some to imagine
that their eyes extinguish waiting for some beacon
to shine from the horizon of their dreams.

5.
Dreams without friends who survive,
without even a common language
in which to aspire. . . . Of those most
gifted at survival, some few become

painters, say, or poets, glimpsing
a world's flawed heart in the mirror
of their own, giving the cunning of
their hands and tongues to those

from whom they learn to show not only
what it was like but what it was—
transfiguring paper into surf
we hear and smell standing there barefoot

where waves lapse into memory, turning
wandering pain into fixed constellations
where an orienting polestar stubbornly burns,
pulling us toward whatever it is our lives become.

THE NIMROD LITERARY AWARDS
The Katherine Anne Porter Prize for Fiction

SECOND PRIZE
LAURA LeCORGNE

Really Good Feet

Now it was November and she'd been there since spring. Her husband called on weekends, wondering when they might return, but Hannah couldn't say. She'd arrived at a point where she'd accept anything—a shadow of longing, the thick weight of duty, loathing would be a fine relief—but all she could summon was a worn fogginess she'd grown accustomed to, which could no longer be blamed on the blanket of heat that lay over the city and probably wouldn't lift until Christmastime. Sometimes she found herself desperate for snow.

Her parents slipped from the room when he called, wandered the halls of their house, pretended not to hear. From time to time, her mother said, "Your voice shifts into neutral when it's Greg on the phone."

He typically waited until Sunday to call, from up at the house in Connecticut. Sometimes she could picture him there, on the other end of the line, in the kitchen, probably, or at his desk upstairs, the phone cradled in his neck, which smelled of sandalwood soap. Mostly she refrained from imagining him at all.

He had come down once that summer, in July, to see the baby for a few days. *Leave him,* her friends admonished, or, *go back,* they said and changed the subject, as though she were viral, as though this sort of trouble might seep into their own lives if they lingered on it for long. They steered the conversation toward other things—their children's sleeping habits, their husbands' professional worries, their wallpapers and topiaries and rugs.

Hannah called her sister Callie in Shreveport every few days. *Leave him,* Callie said. She never said *go back.*

Now it was another Sunday. She dressed the baby and left before her parents woke up. At a bakery on Magazine Street, she bought a newspaper and a boxful of muffins for later. She drove past rental houses, contemplating the notion of solitude, the classified ads spread across the steering wheel like a map. A gum-pink cottage with an orange tree near the front steps, a blue stucco duplex lit bright by the sun. It had been alarmingly hot all November, even for this far south. The baby stirred in her carseat in back. Hannah folded the newspaper and drove off. It seemed that all the little rentals were painted pink or blue or yellow. The sky was white and still.

Long before they bought it, the salt air had faded their house in Connecticut toward a mild, unobtrusive gray, the color of rocks, or wintering birds. The wind off the Sound shredded clouds into long ribbons in the endless blue sky; a fir tree in the yard held snow in its branches all winter. The lawn drifted down to a strip of brown beach where at low tide purple clamshells and seaweed and sometimes an unfortunate eel dried out. It had taken her a year to get used to the rhythm of surf outside their bedroom windows, but now Hannah had trouble falling asleep in the quiet.

It was a plain, airy house, neither very small nor very large, but in the short time they lived there it had grown too close to contain the silences between them, and one day he said that she should take the baby and go to her parents' house for a while, while he thought things through. She ignored the suggestion until he repeated it a few days later. It was early spring when he said it the second time, the windows in the bedroom opened onto the beach. The curtains lifted and fell like loose sails on the air. Hannah told him that she was afraid she might not come back, if he asked her to leave.

"Sure you will," he had said.

She drove away from the rental houses, toward the street where she'd grown up, further in from the river. She parked in her parents' long driveway, the baby asleep in back, a scrap of muffin in her fist, the top of the baker's white box opened on the seat beside her. Hannah lifted the baby from the car and noticed her mother's friend, Deborah, near the front gate, and Julian, who came around to weed the flower beds, bleach moss off the patio bricks, mow the grass every Sunday, as he had since Hannah could remember, there with her. They stood close together, as though they were old friends, and this lifted Hannah's spirits. She'd ask them to come in for breakfast. Her parents would be home from church soon. There were too many muffins in the box.

She waved half a wave with her fingers, the palm of her hand pressed between the baby's shoulder blades, but Deborah and Julian didn't wave back. They walked toward her, still together, she'd always remember, and then Julian handed her a sheet of paper with a telephone number scrawled on a diagonal, she would remember that, too, and told her that Callie had been hurt. Hannah pushed the baby into Deborah's arms because her own began to wobble.

The most cruel thing, she would realize later, was that it happened on a day that seemed plain. So that you could never trust another, so that every day from then on held in its purposeful or dreamy or restful hours the possibility of bottomless grief. But this was a realization years distant, and elusive.

"Where are Helen and Frank?" Deborah asked.

Hannah didn't want her parents to come through the gate. She folded the paper with the telephone number into small squares, walked away, folding and unfolding the paper.

"Where's your mother, honey?" Deborah said again. "Where's Helen right now?"

"At church," Hannah said.

Julian said, "You need to go on inside and call that doctor back."

The doctor asked whether she was a relative, as though she might be trying to pull something off, and when Hannah answered, *yes*, a cool stream of words rolled from his mouth, a tumbling of unimaginable words, about Callie's head and her lungs and her breathing. A bruised heart, he said.

"When will she be awake?" Hannah asked, and the doctor said that they should come up right away.

The kitchen smelled like toast, but there was no comfort in it, as though toast was some kind of joke from another life, which had stopped ten minutes before.

Her throat closed but she didn't cry. She wasn't inclined toward thinking the worst, until the worst was a certainty. Anything could turn itself around. She remembered that her parents would be hungry and began cracking eggs into a bowl. They would be hungry, just like any other Sunday. But they wouldn't be hungry, and she stopped cracking the eggs.

There was a lovely white box full of pastries on the counter, a message from Connecticut on a pad.

Her mother came into the house first. When she opened the front door, Deborah and Julian turned away, toward the dining room, as though pulled by strings. Helen looked at Hannah, her head tipped to the side, a strange half-smile on her face. "What is it," she said, and then her father was there in the hall, navy wool jacket in the crook of his elbow, white cotton shirtsleeves rolled up. "What is it?" Helen said again, and Hannah told it and her father whipped the blue jacket to the floor with a popping sound and said *oh goddamn,* and her mother's arms wrapped tightly around herself, like vines, her waist still narrow as a girl's, as she turned and drifted toward the back of the house.

Hannah had seen her father cry once before, when she was sixteen and they caught her with a boy she thought she would love forever. She looked at her father now and went down the hall, after her mother.

Helen sat on the edge of the sofa in the sunroom. "Maybe she'll be okay," Hannah said. "She's really strong, you know, from work and all. You know, Mom? Maybe she will be." Callie trained racehorses in Shreveport. Her arms and legs were long and tight, her stomach hard and flat.

"No, she won't," Helen said, and Hannah realized that this could be true. Gray light fell through the windows, the disorienting, dusty light that accompanied hot spells in autumn, a colorless light that made the trees bud out just long enough to freeze when the cold came back around. Hannah watched the light drag the color from her mother's face.

"But maybe she will," Hannah repeated. Callie had had accidents before, the boys had, too, back when they were daredevil children. Everything always turned out fine. Both the boys had ropy white scars beneath their chins, where water skis or snow skis had hit. The bottoms of Callie's feet were crisscrossed with lines from shells that had sliced her skin when she jumped too early off the boat once, onto a crumbly shoal. Hannah had been more inclined toward ear infections than stitches as a child. She preferred blue pools, didn't like swimming in the dark water in Bay St. Louis, up near the country house, went quiet and still when she fell off her skis, before whoever was driving the boat noticed and turned back. She always panicked as the boat sped away.

Her mother walked out of the sunroom, toward the kitchen. She returned with a sheet of paper, said, "You need to find your brothers." Her brothers had been traveling, both on the way home that day, one from a cousin's wedding in Nebraska, the other from South America, where he and his wife had gone to shoot birds. They would be between flights, wandering around airports, flipping through magazines or drinking a beer. Helen told Hannah to find them and tell them to come to Shreveport. Then she went upstairs and packed a bag and she and Frank left the house. Her hair was smooth and turned under, tucked behind her ears, like always. Her mother had Grace Kelly hair.

Hannah stood in the hallway, folded the paper with the boys' flight numbers written on it into tight little squares.

The baby slept in a crib upstairs, arms thrown open to the ceiling. Hannah picked her up and sat in a chair. She didn't cry with the baby pressed against her.

People came. She went downstairs. The people looked at her with what appeared to be curiosity and fear, both, on their faces. She walked back up the stairs and locked herself in her parents' bedroom and sat on the edge of the bed.

Her little brother Cotton had a layover in Chicago.

When he was small, Cotton had been filled with curiosity and sweetness and rage. In the neighbor children's yards, or up in the country, he would disappear all of a sudden, then return just as suddenly, his hands filled with mysterious things — hawks' feathers and bleached bits of bone, tiny turtles and frogs, opaque bottles encrusted with sand, triangles of milky green or yellow or brown glass. In his sleep sometimes he cried, sometimes he sang. He threw kisses at strangers in passing cars and sometimes he threw punches for reasons he couldn't explain and once, with perfect aim, he tossed a fork across the kitchen table and hit Hannah in the head, then broke into a spell of inconsolable weeping, so that she had to take him out onto the porch and distract him with airplanes and birds flying overhead, four tiny holes dripping blood on her forehead. He was six then and small for his age. When he was sixteen he got tall and after that he grew beautiful and his anger dropped off him like used-up skin.

Hannah dialed his number and soon Cotton's voice came across the line and Hannah told him and he stopped talking and she heard him begin to cry.

"She flipped the car," Hannah said. "She didn't stay in the car when it rolled over. She went through the windshield."

"Okay," Cotton said.

"She hit her head."

"Okay."

"They're going to operate soon. They said there was pressure on her brain. They're going to try and get it off. They're doing it up in Shreveport, in just a little while."

"Okay," Cotton said.

"They don't know if she can breathe on her own, I guess because of the pressure," Hannah said, and Cotton didn't say anything.

Hannah said, "Get a flight out right now, all right? Tell the people you have to be on the next flight."

"Okay," he said. "I am."

She came from a pull-yourself-up-by-the-bootstraps kind of family and most days couldn't find her shoes.

Turner was in Miami. "Oh, they can fix her, surely they can," he said in his calm, certain voice. Hannah often wondered whether being born first had instilled in him this sturdy capacity for hope, whether his early, spongy years had been filled with so much uninterrupted affection that they had fixed him with the sort of ebullience no one else she had ever known, except on occasion their mother, seemed capable of maintaining. He was an irrepressibly cheerful man. He had made what some people regarded as too much money, playing around with soybean futures and real estate and stocks. Recently he had gotten a little fat. He was capable of talking himself, and others, into unnatural states of happiness. Pain didn't appear to stick to him, though he had had his fair share of grief: a baby lost the day she was born, a college roommate whose safety line broke in the mountains, a girl who moved to Paris without saying why, the only one he wouldn't talk about.

He said he was on his way home, that they'd fly up to Shreveport together. He said to find a babysitter who could spend the night, just one night, that they wouldn't be gone for long, he was sure of it. He said not to worry so much.

Hannah said, "Come get me soon."

Remnants of a storm tossed the plane around in the air and the horizon blackened while the last light fell from the sky. A stewardess came around and handed Hannah a bag for motion sickness, though she hadn't asked for one. Turner said her face looked like chalk.

The hospital was small, four stories high. When the taxi pulled up Turner said, "This can't be the place," and Hannah was filled with fresh dread. The double glass doors swung toward them and they walked into a wall of used air. Their mother and father came from the end of a hall, where they had been waiting; Cotton lagged behind, hands in his pockets. Their mother smiled a regular sort of smile and whispered *do you want to see her* and Hannah said yes. The polished brown floors were a little worn down the middle. A nurse told them to go in one at a time.

Helen said, "She looks different," and pressed a Valium into Hannah's hand.

"I don't think I need this, Mom," Hannah said.

"Well, you might," Helen replied.

White tiles ran up the walls and the floor was white tile, and there were steel boxes and carts scattered about, and the room was very still. A respirator sucked and hissed. Fluorescent tubes in the ceiling cast a shadowless light over the walls and the carts and the floor, and tubes snaked from Callie's arms and mouth, and fresh tubes lay coiled in plastic packages stacked on the carts nearby. Her chest rose and fell with the sound of the machines. What she lay on was not a bed, really, more like a table with sides, higher than a bed, narrower. Her hair hung off the top edge, the new haircut she had told Hannah about the last time they talked, a few days before, maybe three, or four. They had tucked a sheet around her sides, but her arms and shoulders were bare. Her eyelids looked like tiny eggplants, shiny, as though they were wet, but Hannah touched them and they weren't wet. Her mouth turned down at the corners where the tubes had been taped in place. There was a puzzled expression on her face, a quizzical sort of frown. Hannah pushed the hair away from Callie's eyes, drew her finger down her nose. "Please," she said.

At Christmas, a few years before, the last time they were all home at once, Callie stared absently at the bathroom ceiling, flicked her fingers on the surface of the water in the tub where she lay, half-submerged, while Hannah brushed her teeth at the sink. Callie pressed her feet against the tiles on either side of the faucet, turned the hot water on and off with her toes. She said she didn't think she wanted to have children. Her hair fanned out yellow on the water.

"How come you got those really good feet?" she said, after a while. Hannah's toenails were always freshly painted—pink, or sometimes red. Callie's toes angled a little inward, the second longer than the rest by almost half. Her soles were wide and flat.

"Because you got the bosoms," Hannah replied.

Callie said, "Seriously. Why do you think? I mean, they're pretty much perfect."

"Because I am the good child," Hannah said. "Because I want to bear children."

Callie said, "I hate my feet." She turned the water off with her toes and stood, dripping, in the tub. A red scar shaped like a beetle marked the side of one of her breasts, which had been snagged in a crossing-cable strung across a gorge in the Wind River Range. A long, dark line cut slantwise down her thigh, from a snow-skiing accident a few winters before. An elegant white crescent curved above her left eyebrow, where she had been kicked by a racehorse at work.

Air blew cold through the vents in the hospital waiting room. Hannah pulled on a sweater. Nobody said much for a while. Soon two doctors came around and told them that it would take a little longer before the latest tests came back. The one who did most of the talking was short and pale, with hair the color of cement. There was a gap between his bottom teeth, which caused a whistling sound when he said words beginning with an *s* or an *f*. Hannah recognized his voice from the telephone. He paced back and forth in quick, jerky steps while he talked. Before he left, he told Helen and Frank that they could sit with Callie that night, that he'd tell the nurses it was okay. Helen stood up; a silver rosary fell from her lap.

Hannah roamed around in the halls. Beneath the smell of coffee and pine cleaner, and sometimes a sudden drift of vomit, or shit, the hospital held a sweet, cloying odor, like paperwhites kept too long after Christmas.

She went back to the waiting room to find her brothers.

Cotton lay on a green vinyl sofa, staring at the Weather Channel on a muted television mounted high in the corner of the room. Hannah lay down at the other end of the sofa, with Cotton, foot to foot. They looked at the ceiling or at one another and when the double doors leading to the intensive care unit opened, they looked there. Cotton rubbed his feet together. His socks were thick and gray.

"Greg called," he said after a while. "He's coming down. He's worried about you."

"What did you tell him?"

"I told him you were okay."

"Did you tell him to stay in Connecticut?"

"Of course not."

"He's coming down?"

"Yeah."

When Hannah woke the next morning, her neck was stiff and sore. Cotton prodded her with his foot, nodded toward Turner, who smiled while he slept in a chair. Soon their mother and father returned, filled with what seemed like an exaggerated sort of confidence. They had watched Callie through the night and nothing had changed one way or another. Helen knew the names of all the nurses now—Crystal and Sherry and Gretchen and Peg—and asked Hannah if she wanted to meet them, and Hannah said no.

The day was clear with sumptuous pink clouds trimmed in gold. They sat near a picture window. They held cups of coffee in their hands. It seemed that their mother couldn't stop talking, her hands making circles in the air. Whenever Hannah tried to take a drink of the coffee, she had to swallow twice.

The double doors swung open and they looked toward them all at once but it wasn't Callie's doctor coming through the doors. Their mother suggested that they go to the cafeteria and eat some eggs, but nobody got up. She passed around a tin of tiny white mints and rummaged through her purse for gum. Their father sat quietly, watched their mother pass the mints around. The double doors opened again. Callie's doctor walked out and Helen smiled at him. He asked them to come with him into another room. Hannah followed her father, whose white cotton shirt was somehow still fresh. A monogram on the cuff, in blue.

Their father was a modest man, handsomely groomed but not vain. He had worked for the same law firm for over thirty years, though it was hard to tell whether he liked it much. He liked to eat dinner at home around eight o'clock and his shirts pressed with no starch and he liked nine o'clock mass on Sunday mornings. He liked to eat eggs in the kitchen after. Hannah suspected that he was terrified of God. His eyes were the shape and color of burned almonds, from his mother, who had been Cuban and French. When he was nervous, which was rare, he sometimes mixed up his words.

They followed the doctor into a smaller room with chairs lining the walls. Their mother sat down in a chair near the door, her lovely long hands folded in her lap. She looked up at the doctor with a pleasant smile on her face, as though he were telling a story, as though he were a guest at her house. Hannah looked at her mother's hands, her movie star hair. She heard the doctor say a few things about the surgery in his strange halting voice and then she heard him say that Callie was brain dead and she watched as her mother began to age.

"That can't be right," Turner said. Cotton jammed his hands into his pockets, his eyes fixed on the floor.

"How could you even know that for sure?" Hannah's father asked. "No offense, but this hospital's awfully small."

"She can't breathe off the ventilator," the doctor continued. He rocked back and forth on his feet. The need to smack her hand across his face rose up in Hannah like lust.

"We're going to see about flying her home to New Orleans, down to Ochsner, where we know some people," Frank said. "No offense, but we want a secondary opinion."

Helen said, "Second opinion."

The doctor said, "You can unplug her here or you can do it down there, it won't make any difference, is the thing." It seemed to Hannah that the lights overhead might be humming. It seemed that there was a buzzing in the room and that surely it must be coming from the lights. There was a chair behind her father and what happened to him then was not like sitting—his legs simply bent and he was in the chair. Hannah walked out.

"Breathe," Callie had said, holding her head over the toilet, the morning they did the tests. They had gone to the 24-hour Katz & Bestoff on Louisiana Avenue the night before and bought three kits, in pink and lavender and blue boxes, just to be sure, Callie had said. "Your pee has to be brand new and full of those freaked-out hormones you might be making. Don't worry so much or you'll make more. You're probably just worried is all. We have to wait until morning, anyway, so stop pacing like that, okay?" She got into Hannah's bed and soon she was asleep. The next morning Hannah peed into a vial and onto two strips, and when they all came out the same way, she walked into the kitchen and drank a Coke and then she walked to the bathroom and vomited into the toilet.

"Breathe," Callie said, holding her hair back. "Take really big breaths."

Now, behind her, the door closed on the doctor's whistling voice, in the room where her father was in a chair. She walked past the nurses' station and down a bright, empty hallway. At a bank of

elevators she hit the up arrow and soon the doors spread open. A
small, brown-haired nurse smiled at her from the back of the elevator. The walls inside were shiny, some kind of metal, and the elevator was long and wide, for hospital beds and wheelchairs and machines. Hannah pressed the button for the highest floor, but there
were only four floors. She turned toward the metal wall while the
elevator went up and soon heard wild noises that she didn't recognize as something that might come from a person whose mother
had never raised her voice or cried in public or left the house without a lipstick in her purse. From an odd distance, she considered
that her head might have hit the elevator wall once or twice. There
was a hollow sound and she heard herself say, "Watch out, you
might snap a bone." Then the nurse was behind her, holding onto
her arms while she sank down and the nurse sank down with her
while the elevator rose up and up. The nurse reached around her
and pushed the button for the floor from which Hannah had come,
and took her back to her brothers.

Her mother pressed a Valium into her hand. Hannah swallowed it with cold coffee in a styrofoam cup.

She had hated swimming off the boat when they were small.
Rootbeer water, they called it. Their father steered the boat
through thin cuts in the rivers and out into the bay. Every weekend they did this. Callie and the boys dove off the steering bridge.
Sometimes their parents fished for a while, sometimes they sat
in folding chairs and watched the children swim. Hannah liked
swimming pools and clear lakes, water where she could see her feet
kicking five feet down. She walked the perimeter of the boat while
her brothers dove in, climbed out and dove again, brushing past
her, whispering *dipshit,* whispering *loser,* whispering *whatanunbe-
lievablepussy,* until she finally climbed up and dove from the bridge,
the flat water rising to meet her faster than she remembered from
before. She sliced through the first cold layer and the next, colder,
and then the dreadful warm spot where slippery green claws and
brown teeth and fangs might be waiting. She arched her back and
shot toward the surface. Callie dove off the stern and swam out
toward her. "Don't go in anymore," she said, every time.

People from the racetrack where Callie worked drifted
into the hospital, trainers and jockeys and stablehands and a vet,
groomers and a bookie and a gray-haired masseur named Dusty
Rhodes. They whispered together in small groups or in pairs.

Helen had come to know all their names, and steered Hannah around by the elbow, making introductions. One or two looked familiar, from the last racing season, but the rest were strangers to her. Some of them stared and at one point a girl who'd just arrived muttered *Jesus Christ* the first time she looked over at Hannah.

Hannah was a small, dark replica of Callie, and the strangers from the racetrack stared. Maybe they were struck only by similarity or maybe by some new truth about hope, or loss, or maybe they were just afraid, Hannah couldn't tell. She talked with a shy, lanky man, a boy, really, the one her mother thought might be in love with Callie, though no one had told her so. He twisted a magazine in his hands as they spoke. He would call Hannah's house every month or so, for five or six years afterward. "I just wanted to hear her voice," he would say over the phone.

A woman came around, a tag pinned to her chest that read: *Your Hostess, Donna,* and handed Hannah a telephone. Hannah could no longer bend her neck. She held her head straight, held the phone away from her ear. Her husband's voice came steady over the line.

"Cotton told me," he said. "Why didn't you call?"

"I did a few times. I didn't leave a message."

"Well, I tried to get you," he said.

"Cotton said so."

"Where's your cell phone?" he asked.

"Off," Hannah replied.

"It was too late to come by the time I got down here last night," he said.

"It's fine," Hannah said.

"What's going to happen? How are you?"

"Fine," she said.

"I'm at your mother's house. There are lots of people here." he said.

"Could you let the babysitter go then, since you're there?" Hannah said.

He said, "Sure."

Outside in the parking lot it was a plain day. Cars rolled down the street. The sun hung in the sky. A fat woman walked by with a fat brown dog on a red leash; an orderly crushed a cigarette beneath the toe of his shoe; a man on a bench read a book.

Turner and Cotton said they were going to the pound to see about Callie's car.

"I'm coming, too," Hannah said.

"C'mon, no, you're not. You don't want to see that," Turner said, and she stayed behind.

In the family waiting room, their parents talked with a priest. A nurse from the new shift came around swinging a white plastic bag, *Patients Belongings* printed in fancy green script down the side. Hannah took the bag from the nurse and locked herself in a bathroom down the hall and sat on the floor and opened the bag. The warm, grainy smell of horse rose up, and sweat and cigarettes and Chanel No.19. She didn't unfold the clothes. She lifted a few things out with the palms of her hands. Leather boots, pink sweater, jeans. Bracelets, watch, rings.

One of Callie's ring fingers was crushed, most of the skin torn away. They had wrapped it in thick white gauze. Her hands lay on the sheet covering her chest, which rose and fell in time with the machines. Her other fingers seemed fine, which Hannah considered odd. She pulled the watch from the bag and the face spilled glittery onto her lap. She slid two silver rings, pinched almost flat, into her skirt pocket, tied the string and wrapped the bag inside her sweater. In the waiting room she slipped it under a chair. She didn't know yet that the clothes inside were cut jagged up the legs, up the middle, down the back, and would fit together like zippers when she laid them out later, on her bed. She didn't know that she would keep the bag on a high shelf in her bedroom and sometimes take it down and breathe in horse and tobacco and Chanel No.19 until the demented air carried the last of it off.

The hostess called Donna escorted a short, heavy man into the waiting room. He had been driving behind Callie and wanted to know whether he should speak with them. They stood in front of him like children lined up for sweets.

He looked out the window while he spoke, and sometimes he looked at their father. He said that the traffic on the highway had been light, everyone going to church or out to Sunday breakfast, he supposed. "At a right regular speed," he said. "She had those two dogs in the back and one of the dogs went off at something he seen, I couldn't tell what but I seen him bouncing around in the way back and then that dog flies from the window, just like that." He snapped his fingers and Helen jumped. "She had all the windows open, seemed like. It's been good weather here all week. She must've cut the wheel too hard, I guess to miss that dog." He stopped speaking for a while, then, to Frank, said, "I'm sure real sorry to say all this." He told them that the dog that had jumped ran off into the woods, most probably to hide and die, as dogs will. The other dog crawled from where the car rested on its side and sat with him, next to Callie, on the grass at the edge of the road. He said that she was still breathing when the ambulance came.

"She weren't conscious, though," he said. "And I didn't never suspect that she was in no pain."

A front had blown through overnight and cold air pushed past the corners of the hospital, into the parking lot where they stood near a helicopter pad. Sheets of cloud stretched across the sky. Two nurses wearing flight suits wheeled the gurney toward the helicopter, and a man in a white uniform held bags filled with liquid above Callie's head, tubes dangling from a metal pole. At the edge of the parking lot, a young man with beautiful black hair watched as the nurses wheeled Callie toward the helicopter. Hannah remembered him now, though it had been a few years and he was thinner, and pale, as a boy who had made Callie's voice go soft when he walked into a party one night. He had been a student then, in medical school. His face crumpled and his hands went through his hair while the nurses loaded the gurney into the helicopter.

On the night Hannah was married, Callie had paced in front of the windows in the bedroom where they dressed, her reflection slipping watery across the dark window panes. She talked without taking a breath, chewed on the insides of her cheeks.

"You've got lipstick on your teeth," Hannah told her.

"You don't have to marry him, you know," Callie said. She rubbed at her teeth with her ring finger. Hannah stepped into a short tea-colored dress. "I'll help with the baby. I'll help you all the time."

"You live all over the place," Hannah said.

"Being a dad isn't going to turn him into a good guy," Callie said.

"You really need to stop," Hannah had said and Callie walked out of the room, left her alone with her pearls.

The little jet their parents had hired was furnished like a tiny living room, with clubbish chairs and walnut end tables, bolted down. Hannah had never seen such an airplane, though her brothers appeared to know exactly how low to duck when they embarked. Someone had put out a tray piled with sandwiches cut into tiny circles and rectangles and squares, ham and turkey and Swiss cheese, as though it were a party. A sprig of parsley on top, a radish rose. There was a bucket filled with ice and cold bottles of water and orange juice and Cokes. The pilots quietly danced the little plane between wedding cake stacks of clouds, silvery pink and white in the morning sun.

Helen chattered about the nice priest at the hospital in Shreveport and the racetrack masseur whose funny name was Dusty Rhodes. She talked about the doctor who would figure things out when they got home. People flew in from Mississippi and Arkansas and Alabama all the time to see him, she said. From time to time she said *you kids eat a sandwich,* but nobody pulled the cellophane off the tray. Frank looked out the window and rubbed Helen's hand with his fingers.

The doctor in New Orleans had young, soft eyes but his face seemed old. He came into the room and pulled up a chair near them. He was tall and muscular, but had probably never been handsome.

"So it isn't good," he said. "She could've had the accident in the parking lot outside this hospital and I wouldn't have been able to help her." When he said it, his face contained a kindness that changed it to that of a boy. He waited a little while and then asked about her kidneys and liver and eyes.

"Her heart's too damaged to harvest," he said, as though they were talking about fruit trees, or wheat in a field. "But if you could just talk for a while about the rest. If you could talk about it together."

"You can't take her eyes," Frank said, and the doctor explained that it would only be a slice off the top, that it wouldn't change her, not really.

"Let them have her eyes, Dad," Cotton said. It was nearly dark when they left the hospital.

People walked around the house with drinks in their hands. People talked in quiet voices; ice tapped at the sides of their glasses. A man put a drink into Helen's hand and she looked at him and smiled and set it down on a table and wandered off, followed by her sister, who had just arrived from Nebraska. A woman with waxy lipstick placed her palms on Hannah's cheeks. "You're going to be all right," the woman said and Hannah said *thank you* and walked into another room.

Her father sat at the kitchen table, a cigarette in his hand. He had given up smoking a few years before. Hannah took a glass from a cabinet and filled it with water and ice and drank off half the water and filled the glass with scotch.

"Do you want a new drink, Dad?" she asked.

"Not right now, sugar," he said. His elbows rested on his knees. He pulled on the cigarette.

Greg came into the kitchen and said that the baby was asleep and patted Frank on the knee and wound an arm around Hannah's shoulders. No one spoke and soon he said that he was going upstairs for a while. Hannah couldn't move her head without turning her whole body along with it.

A man she'd only met a few times, a friend of her father's, she supposed, wrote out a prescription on a pad he took from the pocket of his dark wool suit. Hannah's old boyfriend, Paul, who had decided to become a priest, drove her to an all-night drugstore and came out after a while with a bottle of pills and a Coke. In the dark car, Hannah wanted to pull him to her and press herself into him and kiss his familiar mouth.

"You have to hold onto God as tight as you can right now, is what you have to do," Paul said, and Hannah didn't want to kiss him anymore. She swallowed a pill with the wine she had brought in a plastic cup from the house. She hadn't brought any stockings down from Connecticut. She did not own a funeral dress.

People filled the house. When she walked into the living room, people looked at her with something resembling expectation on their faces. Her father drank whiskey from a tall glass. He spoke in a regular voice now, and smoked a new cigarette. He made room for Hannah on the sofa and she sat down and leaned into him and when he picked up her hand she cried for a while.

They watched her uncles circle the dining room table. "If my brothers don't stop stuffing those little meatballs into their mouths there's going to be more than one funeral around here this week," her father said.

Later, one uncle offered her a piece of steak on a wooden stick. "Dad said somebody sneezed on those," Hannah whispered, and her uncle laughed, but moved closer to the ham. She sliced a piece of pound cake and took it upstairs, hoping that the baby was awake, standing in the crib, holding onto the side, waiting, but the baby was still asleep when she walked into her old bedroom. Light seeped from beneath the bathroom door. The toilet flushed; water ran in the sink. Hannah pulled the door softly behind her as she left.

In her parents' bedroom, her mother sat on the edge of a chair, her hair at odd angles, like tiny bones. Her hands waved in front of her face, as though she were swatting at flies.

"Hey, Mom," Hannah whispered. She stooped and gathered up her mother's hands.

Her mother said, "I can't do it." The pills from the drugstore had loosened Hannah's neck. Her legs felt rubbery and warm. Soon her brothers came into the room.

Turner said, "The hospital called. They're keeping her there until tomorrow."

"Why?" Hannah asked.

"Until the organ people are done, Hannah," Cotton said, his eyes widening, head tipped toward their mother.

Hannah said, "Oh." She took Helen's purse into the bathroom and shook a Valium into her hand. She swallowed it dry, then took three more from the bottle and tucked them into her bra.

Downstairs, she had the idea that she could understand what all the people wandering through the house might be feeling at once, if she concentrated hard enough. She thought that they might be feeling love and hunger, both. Her neck wasn't stiff anymore. She thought she might lie down for a minute on the powder room floor. She jerked awake sometime later, a pounding at the door. She drank from the faucet at the marble sink and leaned in toward her reflection in the mirror. Her cheeks were flushed, hashed red here and there from the rug. She opened the bathroom door. Her husband stood in the hall.

"I'm going to see her," Hannah said and walked past him. He followed.

"I'll take you," he said.

"No. You don't need to come."

"I'm driving you," he said.

At the foot of the hospital bed Hannah watched a cool shadow of curiosity slide across his face.

"I want you to go back now," she told him. She didn't say that she wanted him to go for good, though she knew that this was the truth. "I'll take a cab home," she said.

The intensive care unit smelled empty, like nothing, like the wind in high mountains often smells. Oxygen pushed through canisters and boxes that expanded and contracted in perfect, even

153

rhythm. There were no clocks on the walls. The nurses wrote on papers stacked in silvery boxes or typed at keyboards, their faces lit by screens. Someone whispered what sounded like *take me* from a few beds over, an ancient woman so thin she appeared blue, her legs curled into her chest. She laughed or whimpered, it was hard to tell which, and then said *Harry oh Harry oh God Harry, oh,* her milky eyes fixed on the ceiling.

The ventilator clicked and pushed and kept color in Callie's cheeks. Tomorrow they would cut into her eyes and her belly and the ventilator would click and hiss while they did it. She wouldn't look any different after, they said.

Her feet were bare and unmarked, her arms and hands were, too. Only her face was changed, and the one finger wrapped in gauze. Tubes of yellow light burned in the ceiling. The ventilator pushed and sucked, the ceiling lights flickered and hummed.

❊ ❊ ❊

White roses will fall across the elegant, dark casket that her brothers have chosen, a blanket of roses, like in a winner's circle. The pallbearers will all have been her lovers once, young and handsome and falling to pieces in their handsome, dark suits. A stranger will sing an Ave Maria alone in the high choir loft while incense burns inside a silver ball on a chain that a priest swings with unspeakable calm as he walks in wide circles around the dark casket. The church will fill with people, pressed together close and stiff, in the pews and in the aisles and at the walls and in the back, near the doors. There will be three priests up on the altar, three. But not until the day after tomorrow.

Now there is a space wide enough to sit on, at the edge of the foot of the bed. Her feet are as they've always been, her arms and legs are, too. The silver thing at the end of a chain will leak smoke into the air, from some kind of incense, while the priest says lovely Latin words. There are tubes taped to the sides of her mouth. She has a puzzled expression on her face, a quizzical sort of frown. There will be a blanket of roses and people, sitting and standing and quiet, but not until the day after tomorrow. Now there is a bed with a space big enough to sit on. Now there is a bed, and the edge of a bed, and the foot of a bed, and feet.

Tia Lupita's Recipe for Raven's Wing Soup

The sisters anoint her body —
throat   breasts   belly
hard-worked hands that shaped

bizcochitos light as cloud-cloth,
tamales with the green, or the red
and her soup of dark secrets.

Who looks for her shadow on cocina walls?
Who takes the wrinkled card from its tin box?

First the herbs:

yerba de la negrita, long as brides' braids;
albacar; and osha of the wild mountain taste:
Chop-and-sear beneath red chiles and salt.

And for the pot:

diced onion, in agua to taste; palmful
of cabbage; pintos (soaked the night before,
then cooked two hours); y stew meat,
but buy only at Tío's Carnicería, el miércoles,
and remember, mija, to ask for the discount!

Everywhere, the room breathes broth.

Now ghost hands reach to the rafters:

Inside the red pouch on the azul string —
Not dried black corn, *ni* amolillo, but
midnight's feather, dipped into the boiling
seven times, until the stock wears sorrow.

Father Martín's white hands at twilight offering
prayers for the dead. Her yellowed cloth
at table. The bent tin spoons. The cracked bowls.

Sopa, comforting throats,
breasts,
belly   this

resurrection   ravenous

                                        soaring.

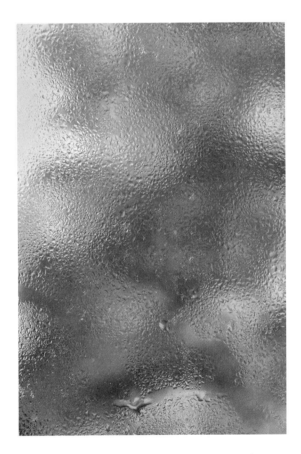

Steven Lautermilch, *Eddy, Easter Morning*, photograph

My Double Death as a Bowl

When I die, I'll come back as a bowl and squat
proudly on the kitchen table, my painted

innards a beauty to behold. No way I'll be salt
and pepper shakers perennially waiting

to serve. And certainly not candlesticks lit
for disappointing holiday dinners. I won't

return as a vegetable knife, or kebob
skewer—I detest pointing anywhere. I'll lie

on my ceramic back, stretch out empty,
and press my two faces into the gleaming

moments between moments which go
slowly. Some days, I might roll an orange

at my navel to say, "Looky here!" Other days,
this glazed eye closed, I'll dream of light

so pure my heart splinters into a calligraphy
of dry riverbed cracks which you absently

finger while wondering if I'm still worth
keeping. But then you'll lift me, admiring

my handmade imperfections, and place me
on a windowsill where you can remember

and also forget. One day, chasing squirrel
shadows, the cat springs and I

tip and shatter. You'll sweep the shards, sad
at how fragile everything is, how nothing

lasts, even me. Until we are both broken,
until nothing more can break, until then.

Charlotte Fein, *Toward Autumn*, oil painting

Love is fertile, Love is fallen leaves

Arrival

The night opened an eyelid and looked at us,
an ancient monster viewing its citizens;
in this night, love yawned, covered her mouth,
yawned again; the car turned as a key
in the streets of night, dawn lay on the other side,
morning was the room beyond, there are many suns,
and many sunrises, in the horizon there are
many dancing suns, one for each of us on earth,
In this night there was the smell of eternal garbage and
slumbering dreams; the moon had the look of a dog slinking
away with a cowardly tail; we awakened from one
dream in mid-air to one on earth.

In Hyderabad parents wait for their children to come,
wait eternally, the knit and purl of arrival and departure
clicking, clicking, clicking in their minds; the hours
here are like gardens with mirrors in which people
come and go, and sow memories that sprout like
entangled weeds covering ground.

The gates open like the covers of a book,
the house waits as an hourglass,
the plot all too familiar:
Love is taken for granted, stoic,
the offer of coffees, teas under smothered sleep,
set unaltered routines, no pleases and thank yous,
no excesses of banal commonalities, no Hallmark realities.

(**News**

I could not have sat still.
A neem leaf however bitter belongs to the neem tree.
Fingers curl back to a palm,
wings lie close to our body,

"Do not come," she said, *"Listen to me. Do not come.*
Do not trouble yourself to come."

The trip was long. There were miles and midnight meals.
There was the Atlantic, the endless sky,
boarding passes, security checks, scrutiny, scans,
aching arms, luggage, tired capture of empty seats
and strained sleep in fetal positions. There was gold in Qatar,
in the duty-free shops, cosmetics, chocolates,
watches, perfumes, crystals and Arabs,
inconvenient restroom stops with carry-ons and child,
the jumble of time, senses, meals; the matrixes, the matrixes.

"We are coming," I said, *"We are coming."*)

Visit

In the hospital the *ayahs* wore red
like the spittle of Goddess Kali,
squatting in corridors, belching,
squelching, clanging bedpans and curses,
bedclothes hung from railings, in her room
no family feuds ceased, weddings were fixed,
visitors sang their poems, a scene from pandemonium,
she so old that desires were like torn kites
wishing for her death that did not come
with the broken hip, grandkids and American accents
foot-diving for blessings, the doctor, old patriarch,
like an aged bulldog took his readings,
aunts hobbled in and out, my father's earnest
manner belying incomprehension.

Departure

She sat up in bed,
skin, sad parchment; white hair,
petal soft, like a lily rising out of the earth;
in her eyes pale milk
of a faded motherhood;
her palms like withered autumn leaves;
she held me as she would a newborn.
What crawls in her blood crawls in mine,
this blood, the sentence it pronounces —
the last light in which to see myself.

*The line "Love is fertile, Love is fallen leaves" comes from the poem
"Moonlight and a Doorstep," by Nguyen Thieu, in *The Women Carry River
Water: Poems by Nguyen Quang Thieu*, translated and edited by Martha Col-
lins and Nguyen Quang Thieu, University of Massachusetts Press, 1997.

Bride

The house was a vase that held us like flowers,
organized us as a family,
the canvas on which we bled our colors,
a canopy, tent, kite, string, rock, water, ship,
glove, tunnel, well, fabric, belly, womb, meadow,
bowl, pen, knife, sword.

We were the sounds in her throat,
we were consonants and vowels,
and we made sense, soon sentences and stories,
and we sailed into the world singing who we are,
others heard us, some did not.

Now, the sounds of hammers, drills, workmen's voices,
medley of Spanish and broken English, radio stations
of Latino beats, strangers in her corridors, peering into her soul,
the kitchen lies bare, stripped of the vinyl tiles,
cement sheets strewn, the borders between rooms gone,

sea.

We adorn the house like a bride to auction her to the highest bidder,
we repair her like trying to repair a woman's hymen making her virgin,
that the world may not see how we've penetrated her body,

how we are fused, that the house is us now,
she is our soul, the daughter who mothered us,
breathed us in and out, strong arms that held us,
womb, boat, passageway, inside of the sun,
volcano, desert land, vortex, nucleus of the atom,

is now an eye-blink, we will be gone from her site/sight,
we the marauders who flourished in her wealth.

Filament

Early evening. The only time of day the seeds
from a tree you'll plant in ten years are visible,
floating on the wind. People rise from their dinners
to watch from their second-story windows,
telling their kid to quit it already with the Abbado,
this is the time to improvise if ever there were,
just let the keys take you where they will. Peering
through a buttery Sauvignon with a breadcrumb
sieve bottomed in the glass, at contrails pinking
as they dissolve, at a string of geese unspooling
from the giant geeseball Dahl should have invented.
At the spider webs, spilled light & sand-dollar scaffolding,
glistening on the grass, on the boxwoods, a host
of starry parachutes. Remember the American
caught crossing into North Korea in your prayers
tonight. Remember those who have yet to find
what they wish to die for, but spend their lives
looking, like Jonah. They're the ones who in days
long past would bring everything they could
to the temple to be burned, once a year, to thank God
for everything they had. I love them for their faith,
for handing down Isaiah to me after three thousand
years, for somehow, miraculously, keeping his words
unchanged. The sound of the wakes their lives leave
behind them is like leaves stirring in their sleep to let go,
like the murmur of some lost thrush, though
you've never seen one. The evening will drown itself
in itself, like yesterday, the questions you've asked returned
as questions. I'm waiting for you to take your first breath,
tonight, to awaken with a verse on your lips, a verse you read
as a child, to move so easily through the world outside
that everyone's clustered around their windows, gawking
at the translucent body tending to the last shoots of light.

KATHRYN NUERNBERGER

Still Life

How hard it is to see clearly.

Take this grape. It's violet,
but not quite, magenta,
but not quite.

More the amethyst night
of a lighted bridge
when there's a bit of dawn
and you've been out late,
lying in the park next to
your best girl friend,
and you've gotten
that rustling feeling out
of your chest for a minute.

Only not quite.

More the color of her coffin
with its deep-wood shine
carried under the stained glass
as the choir sings, but no sound,
as you sing, but no sound.

More the shade of that perfect quiet.

Only not quite so perfectly round,
or perfectly dark, but reflecting
the white light of morning
on its shriveling skin
as one last thing that was hers
passes the plum shadow,
the wrinkled fig, of your pursed lips.

And now where there was fruit,
there are thorns. Not thorns
exactly, but woody fingers,

green tattered ends without name,
more green than yellow, more
green than brown, but not
green, not exactly green.

Steven Lautermilch, *Torn paper*, photograph

The Wallow Variations

Before the stock market crashes for good,
and we're left defending our small patch of pride
permit me to digress—
in a word, to wallow in excess.

Fill your pinched cheeks with warm air, a tuba
slowly blowing out: *Wall-ow*.

The laws against foolery have been overthrown
by yodeling bands of jobless brokers.
Follow their lead and put your stock
in the weightless wings of mission swallows.

Only ascetics eat aspic when marshmallows abound.
Better to dine on melons, Mallomars, and hot syrup waffles.
Look at the pigs wallowing in mud.
Do you still think them awful?

Imagine wrapping yourself in whatever you love—
Viennese waltzes, Whitman, Van Gogh.
(Behold the beautiful walleyed girl,
how her Picasso eyes wander all directions.)

There is no end to it, once you wade in. Your body
is wired for the perfect expression of yellow—
sunflowers, jonquils, full moonlight, champagne.
Wear them, worship them, ride over them in a barrel.

A wanton kiss is your Buddha blossoming.
Oh, my worried friend, take my word.

Elegy Without Words

Marie Smith Jones said good-bye to no one, there being no one left
who knew the Eyak word for leave-taking.

She died in her sleep in the first month of a cold,
young year. With her went a place, and the history
of a place, as happens when languages disappear,
as they do, twice with each moon.

Crushed by an army's boot, absorbed by a larger world,
there are no words for what's gone missing —
Gods and songs and ways of cooking fish.

In Queensland, a tribe with no saying for left or right
beheld one another as points on a compass. To the north,
the Eyak people, believing trees and birds were bound,
formed a single sound to mean leaf and feather.

Mourn the lost consonants, the cloistered vowels.
Mourn Marie Smith Jones, the last of her tribe
to put breath to word, word to wind.

Weep for Wappo, Barbareno, Akkala Sami, Ubykh —
the echoes from eastern Russia,
the fallen sighs of the Southern Hemisphere.

Reading As I Lay Dying

for JGW, 16 June 1939-30 March 2010

I have been reading *As I Lay Dying*
For the very first time. It's great. I realize
Telling you this is a lot like saying
To me, "His *Lear*'s quite good; I may be trying
His *Hamlet*, too, one of these days."
Perhaps what I've been doing is re-reading?

You've never been one for the little lies
Professors tell to go on seeming knowing,
Our habit from the years of barely staying
Ahead of students, and with friends, evading
Attention to the holes left in our reading.
What we don't know is not what we like saying.

But these spring days as light keeps growing
Brighter on the bed where you lie reading
There's not much time for little or big lying
Between you and all of us you're leading
On toward the darkness at the end of trying
Beyond anything we can be truly knowing.
It's a different kind of truth you're wanting
As you lie reading.

True that we all will take the road you're taking.
True that it's yours alone you must be walking,
Hobbling, now, with the clotting and the swelling.
These are not the truths that you are wanting.

We bring instead our stories of your teaching
And set you into stories of our teaching,
Ignoring cancer, focusing on honor,
As if we all were characters in Homer.
Not asking questions none of us can answer,
You'd rather speak of the endowed professor
Who in an institutional forever
In academic deeds will always name you.

The phone rang yesterday while we were talking,
And knowing that a friend had tried to reach you,
You picked up, listened, answered the cold-caller,
Your voice gentle, final, and forbearing,
"Sir, I cannot help you."
It was well said, but not for saying to you.

"He was my hero," you said the day you told me,
Remembering your surgeon father's dying.
He too gives his name to a professor.
You held his scalpel hand and told him,
"You are the best." Breathless with emphysema,
Self-knowing, irritable, not in terror,
"That's a god-damned lie," he gathered voice to say,
His final words.

From what I know of you and him
It may in some ways have been an error
But you were not lying.

Jim, we are not lying.

10 March 2010

ABOUT THE AUTHORS

MARK AIELLO is a New York City-based poet and executive in operations management for a Fortune 500 company. His work has appeared in *Poetry*, *The Southampton Review*, *Evansville Review*, *Antietam Review*, and *Atlanta Review*, among other journals, as well as in the anthologies *180 More* and *Naming the World*.

USHA AKELLA, the author of two books of poetry, moved to the U.S. from India in 1993 and now lives in Austin, Texas. She has read widely in poetry festivals, museums, cultural and educational institutions worldwide. Her work has appeared or is forthcoming in U.S. and Indian-based journals such as *The Bitter Oleander*, *Drunken Boat*, *The Crab Orchard Review*, *Indian Literature*, and *Kavya Bharati*. She launched the Poetry Caravan to provide free poetry workshops and readings to disadvantaged people.

HARRY BAULD is from Medford, Massachusetts. He won the *New Millennium Writings* Poetry Award in 2008, and his poems have appeared in *The Southeast Review*, *Whiskey Island*, *Southern Poetry Review*, and *Deliberately Thirsty (UK)*, among other journals. He is a former wine columnist and boxing coach and currently teaches at Horace Mann School in New York.

TERRY BLACKHAWK is the author of *Body & Field*, *The Dropped Hand*, and *Escape Artist*, which won the 2002 John Ciardi Prize, as well as two chapbooks. Her poems have appeared in journals such as *Marlboro Review*, *Michigan Quarterly Review*, *Artful Dodge*, *Florida Review*, and *Borderlands*. Her work is in many anthologies, most recently *When She Named Fire: Contemporary Poems by American Women*, and she has twice been a finalist for *Nimrod*'s Pablo Neruda Poetry Prize. The founding director of Detroit's InsideOut Literary Arts Project, she lives in Detroit, Michigan.

ONUR CAYMAZ, one of the leading names among the youngest generation of Turkish writers, was born in Istanbul. His works have been published in *Adam Sanat*, *Adam Öykü*, *Poetikus*, *Öteki-Siz*, *Cumhuriyet Kitap*, and other journals. His first poetry collection, *Kah ve Rengi*, won the Orhon Murat Arıburnu Poetry Competition in 2000. His poetry anthology, *Bak Hâlâ Çok Güzelsin* (*Look, You're Still Very Beautiful*), won the 2005 Behçet Aysan Poetry Award. He is also the author of award-winning short stories.

MORRIS COLLINS, a Boston native, received his M.F.A. from The Pennsylvania State University, where he now teaches English and rhetoric. His work has recently appeared in *Rattle*, *Mid-American Review*, *In Posse Review*, *The Magazine of Speculative Fiction*, *Grasslimb*, *Neon*, and *Rain Taxi*.

PAMELA DAVIS is a poet living in the flammable hills above Santa Barbara, California. As a writer and editor specializing in health and medicine, she authored two nonfiction books. She now concentrates on poetry, splitting her time between Paris and California. Her work appears or is forthcoming in *The Evansville Review, Pearl, Poem, Quiddity, Red Cedar Review, The South Carolina Review, Southern Humanities Review,* and other journals. She is at work on her first book of poems.

TODD DAVIS teaches creative writing, environmental studies, and American literature at Penn State University's Altoona College. His poems have won the Gwendolyn Brooks Poetry Prize and recently appeared in *The Iowa Review, The Gettysburg Review,* and *Indiana Review.* He is the author of three books of poems, *The Least of These, Some Heaven,* and *Ripe.* His work has been featured on Garrison Keillor's *The Writer's Almanac* and in Ted Kooser's newspaper column *American Life in Poetry.*

DEBORAH DENICOLA's memoir, *The Future That Brought Her Here,* was recently released from Nicholas Hays/Ibis Press. A collection of poetry, *Original Human,* is forthcoming in 2010 from WordTech Press. She edited the anthology *Orpheus & Company: Contemporary Poems on Greek Mythology.* Previous books include *Where Divinity Begins* and three chapbooks, most recently *Inside Light.* Among other awards, she has received an NEA Fellowship. Her poetry is published widely in journals and online.

LARS ENGLE, chair of the Department of English at The University of Tulsa, writes mainly for scholarly publications, focusing on Shakespeare and other early modern English dramatists and on contemporary South African literature, especially the fiction of Nadine Gordimer and J. M. Coetzee.

KATE FETHERSTON's poems have appeared in journals including *North American Review, Hunger Mountain, Nimrod,* and *Third Coast.* A finalist for *Nimrod*'s Pablo Neruda Prize in 2008, she has received an individual artist's grant from the Vermont Council on the Arts and several Pushcart nominations. She is a psychotherapist in private practice in Montpelier, Vermont.

NINA FORSYTHE has an M.F.A. from Bennington and her poems, translations, and reviews have been published in a variety of magazines, including *5 AM, Chiron Review, Taproot, Puerto del Sol,* and *Review Revue.* She has been nominated for a Pushcart Prize and was awarded the 2010 *Backbone Mountain Review* Poetry Prize. She conducts creative writing workshops for students of various ages in western Maryland.

ED FRANKEL's poetry has appeared in *Fugue, Confluence, Dogwood: A Journal of Poetry and Prose*, and other journals. Among other awards, he won first prize in the *Confluence* 2003 poetry contest, the 2008 *New American Review* Chapbook contest, the 2009 *New Millennium Writings* Poetry contest, and the 2010 Little Red Tree Press poetry contest. His chapbook, *When the Catfish Are In Bloom: Requiem for John Fahey*, was nominated for The PEN Center USA Literary Award and the California Book Award. His chapbook *People Of The Air* was published by New American Press.

DAVID GIBBS's poems have appeared recently or are forthcoming in the *Columbia Poetry Review, Mayday*, and *Eclipse*. He works for the Wexner Center for the Arts and lives in Columbus, Ohio.

ARDA GÖKÇER, translator of Onur Caymaz's poem "sister of pain," studied marketing in the U.S., where she spent seven years traveling and discovering the country. She also worked in London as a freelance journalist for a Turkish literature publication. She now lives in Istanbul and works for an advertising agency as the foreign accounts director.

JESSICA HARMAN's third chapbook of poems, *Take Me As I Am*, was published in 2010 by Propaganda Press. Her poems have recently appeared in *Karamu, Spillway*, and *Bellevue Literary Review*. She lives in Haverhill, Massachusetts.

REBECCA HAZELTON has poems published or forthcoming in *Pleiades, Drunken Boat, FIELD*, and *webConjunctions*.

GINDY ELIZABETH HOUSTON's work has appeared in *The Smoking Poet* and *New Millennium Writings*; two of her poems received honorable mention in *New Millennium Writings'* 2008 Awards for Fiction, Poetry, and Nonfiction.

AMORAK HUEY, after 15 years as a newspaper reporter and editor, teaches writing at Grand Valley State University in Michigan. He has an M.F.A. from Western Michigan University and his poems can be found in *Crab Orchard Review, Subtropics, Gargoyle, Controlled Burn*, and other journals.

LUKE JOHNSON holds an M.F.A. from Hollins University. Recent work has appeared or is forthcoming in *Beloit Poetry Journal, Crab Orchard Review, The Greensboro Review, Passages North*, and *Best New Poets 2008*. He lives in the Blue Ridge Mountains of Virginia.

LYDIA KANN, a writer, visual artist, and psychotherapist, has published stories in *Threepenny Review* and *Nimrod International Journal*, where she received Honorable Mention for the 2003 Fiction Prize. She also has been a finalist for many fiction prizes, including for *Glimmer Train*, *Iowa Review*, *Black Warrior Review*, Kore Press, *New Letters*, and *The Journal*. She has been awarded residencies at the Djerassi Resident Artist Program, the Norman Mailer Writers Colony, and the Julia and David White Artist Colony.

DAN KELTY is a high school Spanish teacher in St. Louis, Missouri, where he lives with his wife and two children. He has been previously published in *MARGIE*, *Steam Ticket*, *Pure Francis*, and *Natural Bridge*. A forthcoming poem will be published in *Sleet* e-zine. He was selected as a finalist for the *Nimrod* Poetry Contest in 2007.

KATIE KINGSTON is the author of three poetry collections: *Unwritten Letters*, *El Rio de las Animas Perdidas en Purgatorio*, and *In My Dreams Neruda*. She is the recipient of the 2010 W.D. Snodgrass Award for Poetic Endeavor and Excellence and has recently completed a fellowship residency at the Fundación Valparaíso in Mojácar, Spain. Currently she lives and writes in Trinidad, an area known as the coal fields, located in the foothills of the Sangre de Cristo Mountain Range.

JOHN KNOEPFLE, poet, translator, and professor of literature, has published poems and translations in major collections of Latin American, Chinese, and American literature. He has published over 16 books of his own poetry. He is known not only for his poetry and translations but also for his research and private collection of Americana, especially the American West.

BRANDON KRIEG's poems have appeared or are forthcoming in *The Iowa Review*, *Shenandoah*, *The Massachusetts Review*, *Seneca Review*, and many other journals. He lives in Chicago, where he is an instructor at DePaul University.

MARGARITE LANDRY's work has appeared in the *Provincetown Arts Magazine*, *Bellingham Review*, *Vermont Literary Journal*, and *Pisgah Review*. Her novel-in-progress, *Blue Moon*, won the James Jones First Novel Fellowship in 2008. Her short fiction has been selected for honorable mention in the *New Millennium* Awards 2009, runner-up for the Tobias Wolff Award 2008, and finalist for the Howard Frank Moser Short Fiction Prize 2009. She teaches professional writing at Fitchburg State College in Massachusetts.

LAURA LeCORGNE holds an M.F.A. from the Bennington Writing Seminars. Her work has appeared in *Black Warrior Review*, *Colorado Review*, and *Mississippi Review*, among other journals. She lives in New Orleans.

ANGIE MACRI received an M.F.A. from the University of Arkansas at Fayetteville. Her work has been published in journals including *Arts & Letters, Fugue, New Orleans Review,* and *Southern Indiana Review,* and was featured in *Spoon River Poetry Review.* She has been awarded an individual artist fellowship from the Arkansas Arts Council.

TOM MOORE, who holds a Ph.D. from the University of Chicago, has taught for 25 years in the history of culture at Western Washington University. In addition to his academic publications, his poetry has appeared in *Rhino, St Petersburg Review, Melic Review, Mystic River Review, The Fairfield Review,* and other journals.

COLLIER NOGUES was recently the Fishtrap Writer-in-Residence in Wallowa County, Oregon. Her first book will be published in Spring 2011 by Four Way Books, and poems of hers have recently appeared or are forthcoming in *Pleiades, Jubilat, Barrow Street, Washington Square,* and *Third Coast.*

KATHRYN NUERNBERGER is the editor of *Quarter After Eight* and recipient of a 2010 AWP Intro Journals Award. Her work has appeared in journals including *Mid-American Review, Conduit, Barrelhouse,* and *The Literary Review.*

JUDE NUTTER's poems have appeared in numerous journals including *Alaska Quarterly Review, Atlanta Review, Crazyhorse, Indiana Review, The Missouri Review, Notre Dame Review,* and *Stand (UK).* She is the recipient of several awards and grants, including two Minnesota State Arts Grants, a McKnight Fellowship, the Robinson Jeffers Tor House Prize, and the *Missouri Review* Editors' Prize. Her books include *Pictures of the Afterlife* and *The Curator of Silence* and *I Wish I Had A Heart Like Yours, Walt Whitman,* which won the 2007 and 2010 Minnesota Book Awards in Poetry.

SUE PACE has been writing for over thirty-five years. Thus far she has had one novel published (*The Last Oasis*) and many short stories, which may be found in journals such as *CALYX, Skive, Kalliope, Other Voices, Phoebe,* and now *Nimrod.*

LINDA PASTAN's 13th book of poems, *Traveling Light,* will be published by Norton in January of 2011. She was Poet Laureate of Maryland from 1991 to 1995 and has been a finalist twice for the National Book Award. In 2003 she won the Ruth Lilly Poetry Prize.

DOUG RAMSPECK's poetry collection, *Black Tupelo Country,* was selected for the 2007 John Ciardi Prize for Poetry. His chapbook, *Where We Come From,* is published by March Street Press. His poems have appeared in journals such as *Prairie Schooner, West Branch, Third Coast, Northwest Review*, and *Hayden's Ferry Review*. He was awarded an Ohio Arts Council Individual Excellence Award for 2009. He directs the Writing Center and teaches creative writing at The Ohio State University at Lima.

SHANNON ROBINSON's work has appeared or is forthcoming in *Crab Creek Review, Gargoyle, Whiskey Island, Sycamore Review*, and *Sou'wester*. In 2009 she won the *Crab Creek Review* Editors' Prize, and this year another story was chosen by Peter Ho Davies as a Runner-Up for *Sycamore Review*'s Wabash Prize in Fiction. She is a contributing editor at *River Styx*, and this fall will be starting the second year of an M.F.A. in fiction at Washington University. She currently lives in Saint Louis.

WILLIAM PITT ROOT's work from *The New Yorker, The Nation, Atlantic*, and nine collections has been translated into over twenty languages, broadcast over Voice Of America, and funded by the Guggenheim and Rockefeller Foundations, National Endowment for the Arts, and US/UK Exchange Artists program. *White Boots: New and Selected Poems of the West* is Root's most recent collection. *Welcome, Traveler: Selected Early Odes of Pablo Neruda* is forthcoming.

MARTIN SHEEHAN, co-translator of Georg Trakl's "De Profundis," earned his Ph.D. in Germanic Literatures and Languages from the University of Virginia. He has written on the dramatic language of Carl Sternheim, translated in the field of musicology, and taught German studies and comparative literature seminars at universities in both Germany and America.

DONNY SMITH, translator of Onur Caymaz's poem "someone," teaches at a high school in Istanbul. His collection of Lâle Müldür translations, *I Too Went to the Hunt of a Deer*, was published in 2008. His translation, with Abbas Karakaya, of Cemal Süreya's *Üvercinka* is scheduled to be published in 2010. His own collection of poetry, *Was Gone and Has Gone and Was Gone*, appeared in 2008.

ANITA SULLIVAN divides her creative life between music and literature. She has published two books of creative nonfiction, one on the Greek island of Ikaria and one on the philosophy of piano tuning. Her poetry chapbook is *The Middle Window* (Traprock, 2008); Airlie Press will publish a full-length collection, *Garden of Beasts*, in 2010.

RICHARD TERRILL is the author of a collection of poems, *Coming Late to Rachmaninoff*, winner of the Minnesota Book Award, and two books of creative nonfiction, *Fakebook: Improvisations on a Journey Back to Jazz* and *Saturday Night in Baoding: A China Memoir*. He has been awarded fellow ships from the National Endowment for the Arts, the Wisconsin and Minnesota State Arts Boards, and the Bread Loaf Writers' Conference. He has taught as a Fulbright professor in China, Korea, and Poland, and now teaches in the M.F.A. program at Minnesota State University, Mankato.

DAVID THACKER is currently studying poetry as an M.F.A. candidate at the University of Idaho. Poems of his have appeared or are forthcoming in *MARGIE, American Poetry Journal,* and *Blood Orange Review*. He lives in Moscow, Idaho, with his wife and daughters.

FRANCINE MARIE TOLF recently published a memoir, *Joliet Girl*, and a full-length collection of poems, *Rain, Lilies, Luck*, with North Star Press of St. Cloud. Her essays and poems have been published in numerous journals, including *Water-Stone, Mudlark, MARGIE,* and *Southern Humanities Review*. She has received grants from the Minnesota State Arts Board; the Barbara Deming/Money for Women Foundation; Blacklock Nature Sanctuary; the Loft Mentor Series; and the Elizabeth George Foundation.

GEORG TRAKL (1887-1914) was born in Salzburg, Austria, and is often considered one of the most important figures of Austrian Expressionism. Trakl's work was one of the main catalysts for Robert Bly and James Wright's "deep imagism" movement in American poetry in the late 1950s and early 1960s.

DAVID TROUPES's first collection, *Parsimony*, was published in 2009 by Two Ravens Press. A native of Massachusetts, he currently lives in Yorkshire, England, with his wife, where he works in social housing.

JAMES VALVIS has poems or short stories forthcoming in *Chiron Review, Confrontation, Green Hills Literary Lantern, Hurricane Review, Minotaur, New Laurel Review, New York Quarterly, Pearl, RATTLE, Slipstream, Southern Indiana Review, Timber Creek Review,* and other journals. He lives in Washington State with his wife and daughter.

MARK WAGENAAR has recently been teaching film and poetry at the University of Virginia and Sweet Briar College. His poems have been accepted or published by a wide variety of magazines, including *Subtropics, Southern Review, South Carolina Review, North American Review, Poetry East,* and *Tar River Poetry*. He is beginning his Ph.D. in poetry at the University of Utah.

MARGARET WALTHER is a retired librarian from the Denver metropolitan area and a member of Columbine Poets, a statewide organization to promote poetry in Colorado. She has taught workshops and has been a guest editor for *Buffalo Bones*. She has published in many journals, such as *Connecticut Review* and *Quarterly West*, and has a poem forthcoming in *A cappella Zoo*.

KAROL M. WASYLYSHYN, President of Leadership Development Forum, is a clinical and consulting psychologist specializing in leadership development. In addition to her professional writing, she is currently working on a leadership book based on the core behaviors she has observed in business executives over the last 30 years. Original case examples of these behaviors are presented through her poetry.

ANDREA L. WATSON's poetry has appeared in *Runes, Ekphrasis, Cream City Review, Subtropics, The Dublin Quarterly, International Poetry Review, Nimrod*, and *Memoir (and)*. Her show, *Braided Lives: A Collaboration Between Artists and Poets*, founded with artist Seamus Berkeley, was inaugurated by the Taos Institute of Arts and has traveled to San Francisco, Denver, and Berkeley. She is co-editor of *Collecting Life: Poets on Objects Known and Imagined*.

SARAH M. WELLS is the author of the chapbook *Acquiesce*, which won the 2008 Starting Gate Award from Finishing Line Press. Her poems have appeared or are forthcoming in *Christianity & Literature, JAMA, Windhover, The Fourth River, The New Formalist, Relief*, and elsewhere. She is the Administrative Director of the low-residency M.F.A. Program at Ashland University, where she serves as Managing Editor for both the Ashland Poetry Press and *River Teeth: A Journal of Nonfiction Narrative*.

WILLIAM WRIGHT, co-translator of Georg Trakl's "De Profundis," is the author of a full-length poetry collection, *Dark Orchard*, winner of the 2005 Breakthrough Poetry Prize and published by Texas Review Press. His chapbook, *The Ghost Narratives*, was published by Finishing Line Press in 2008. Wright's poetry has recently been published in *North American Review, AGNI, Colorado Review, Indiana Review, Beloit Poetry Journal, Southern Poetry Review*, and *Texas Review*, among other literary journals.

KATHRYN DUNLEVIE'S work has been featured in *The New York Times*, the *San Francisco Chronicle*, the *San Jose Mercury News*, and *Artweek*, as well as internationally in *La Fotografia Actual*, *Art of England*, and *Profifoto*. Her work is shown internationally and has been included in exhibitions at Belgravia Gallery and Vertigo in London, Studio Thomas Kellner in Germany, Gallery TPW in Toronto, as well as at Washington, D.C.'s Art Museum of the Americas, Michael Mazzeo Gallery in New York, and others.

CHARLOTTE (CHERI) FEIN, poet and painter, lives and works in New York City. She conceived and edited (1973-6) *Coda: Poets and Writers Newsletter*, and has published her poetry in *American Poetry Review*, *Partisan Review*, and elsewhere. She has exhibited her paintings in the Maxwell Galleries in San Francisco, Bergdorf Goodman in New York City, the Juried Plaza Art Show in Kansas City, and other exhibit spaces.

KEVIN HARDIN is a sculptor and painter. Several of his pieces were included in the book *500 Animals in Clay*. He is represented in Tulsa by Joseph Gierek Fine Art.

MARY HARGROVE was an investigative reporter for 32 years. She is past president and chair of Investigative Reporters & Editors. She was awarded the grand prize Robert F. Kennedy Award and the Casey Journalism medal. She also received a lifetime achievement award from the Tulsa Press Club.

COOKIE JOHNSON is an artist and chef who lives in Colorado.

MANLY JOHNSON is a poet, teacher, and visual artist. He was *Nimrod*'s poetry editor for many years. His latest volume of poetry is *Holding onto What Is: New and Selected Poems*.

STEVEN LAUTERMILCH is a poet and photographer. His recent poems and photos have received prizes from *Atlanta Review*, *Carpe Articulum Literary Review*, *Kakalak*, and the W. B. Yeats Society of New York. His chapbook, *Fire Seed & Rain*, won the 2008 Longleaf Press chapbook competition and received an honorable mention for the Jean Pedrick Award from the New England Poetry Club.

JOHN MILISENDA's photography has appeared in over 125 shows and in publications including *Smithsonian* and *The New York Times*. His work is in the permanent collections of New Orleans Museum of Art, the Museum of Modern Art, and the Bibliothèque Nationale. He is currently working on a photography book of his family.

DANI NEFF is an twelve-year-old student at The Tulsa Girls Art School Project.

ALICE LINDSAY PRICE, who died in 2009, was a poet, painter, and naturalist, and the author of *Cranes: The Noblest Flyer* and *Swans of the World*.

LESLIE RINGOLD is a public defender, poet, and photographer. She lives, works, and plays in Venice, California.

ANNE THOMPSON, who died in 2004, was a widely recognized photographer, in addition to her work as Court Administrator for the City of Tulsa.

MARK WEISS, an ophthalmologist in Tulsa, Oklahoma, is an award-winning photographer.

ABOUT THE JUDGES

MOLLY PEACOCK, judge for *Nimrod*'s 2010 Pablo Neruda Prize for Poetry, is a poet and a creative nonfiction writer. She is the author of six books of poetry, including *The Second Blush* and *Cornucopia: New & Selected Poems*. Among her other works are *How To Read A Poem and Start A Poetry Circle* and a memoir, *Paradise, Piece By Piece*. She is the co-editor of *Poetry in Motion: One Hundred Poems from the Subways and Buses*, a collection arising from the popular program Poetry in Motion, placing poems on placards in subways and buses, of which she was an originator. She was an honorary fellow at The Johns Hopkins University, served as Poet-in-Residence at The American Poets' Corner in New York City, and has received awards from the New York Foundation for the Arts, the National Endowment for the Arts, and the Woodrow Wilson Foundation. She lives in Toronto.

DAVID WROBLEWSKI, judge for *Nimrod*'s 2010 Katherine Anne Porter Prize for Fiction, grew up in rural central Wisconsin, not far from the Chequamegon National Forest, where his mother raised and trained dogs and where his acclaimed first novel, *The Story of Edgar Sawtelle*, is set. At the University of Wisconsin, he became fascinated with the art of making software and earned a degree in computer science. He completed an M.F.A. in creative writing from the Warren Wilson M.F.A. Program for Writers. Writer and software designer, he is also a photographer of black and white landscapes. Over the years he has lived in La Crosse, Wisconsin, Minneapolis, Minnesota; and Austin, Texas. He makes his home in Colorado with the writer Kimberly McClintock.

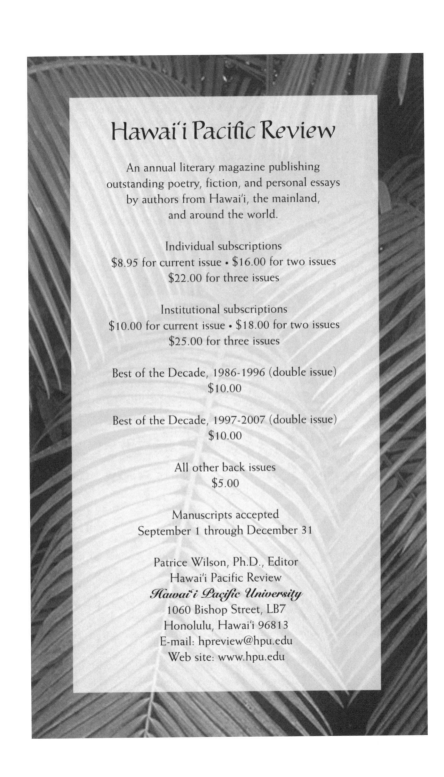

Hawai'i Pacific Review

An annual literary magazine publishing
outstanding poetry, fiction, and personal essays
by authors from Hawai'i, the mainland,
and around the world.

Individual subscriptions
$8.95 for current issue • $16.00 for two issues
$22.00 for three issues

Institutional subscriptions
$10.00 for current issue • $18.00 for two issues
$25.00 for three issues

Best of the Decade, 1986-1996 (double issue)
$10.00

Best of the Decade, 1997-2007 (double issue)
$10.00

All other back issues
$5.00

Manuscripts accepted
September 1 through December 31

Patrice Wilson, Ph.D., Editor
Hawai'i Pacific Review
Hawai'i Pacific University
1060 Bishop Street, LB7
Honolulu, Hawai'i 96813
E-mail: hpreview@hpu.edu
Web site: www.hpu.edu

Superstition Review

The Online Literary Magazine
at Arizona State University

We are now accepting submissions
of fiction, poetry, creative nonfiction, and
art for Issue 6 to be launched November
2010. Visit **www.superstitionreview.com**
to read submission guidelines.

Some of our past issues include:

Adrian C. Louis, Barbara Kingsolver,
Billy Collins, Brian Cohen, Brian Doyle,
Carol Ann Bassett, Cary Holladay,
Daniel Orozco, Deborah Bogen, Edith
Pearlman, Elizabeth Searle, Jane
Bernstein, Jim Daniels, Kelli Russell
Agodon, Leslie Epstein, Michael S.
Harper, Michelle Menting, Nin Andrews,
Sherman Alexie, Sherril Jaffe and more!